I0519102

Play Therapy

The Ultimate Guide to Cultivating Emotional Balance, Reinforcing the Parent-Child Connection, and Enhancing Social Interaction in Everyday Life

Table of Contents

Introduction

In psychology, counseling, and psychotherapy, an existing approach uses the power of play therapy to heal, communicate, and change lives. Specialists and health professionals use this approach often to improve the lives of individuals, families, and communities. It is called "Play Therapy," an innovative and unique method of therapy that uses ethically approved therapeutic techniques to create a reflective and learning avenue for growth and emotional well-being in adults and children alike.

This book focuses on using play therapy with children, young adolescents, and adults. It goes on to help you understand the need for a close relationship between parents and their children, how to build emotional bridges and maintain unimpeded communication that will bring anything that could be out of alignment to your attention as soon as it happens.

With chapters dedicated to helping you understand the intricacies of play therapy, its theoretical foundations, practical applications, and transformative possibilities, this book has the information to empower you with knowledge on play therapy.

You won't just be preparing to read a book; you'll be preparing to embark on a journey exploring play therapy fundamentals. Learning the language of play therapy is a task of its own as it's the primary language used by kids in their developmental stages, and you'll learn to understand their innermost thoughts and emotions without verbalization.

You'll see how play therapy allows children and young adolescents to express themselves in ways that transcend words. You'll discover that play serves as a gateway to healing, growth, understanding, empathy, developing a sense of responsibility, and helping to facilitate the exploration and resolution of emotional, psychological, and stress-related challenges.

With a wealth of knowledge, theories, practical strategies, and hands-on tips and activities, this is a comprehensive guide to the world of play therapy. Written using simple language and for easy assimilation, this book will transform the minds of parents, caregivers, and professionals searching for guidance with rich knowledge on therapeutic techniques and strategies to employ in dealing with children and adolescents.

With the turn of each page, you will gain more knowledge and appreciation for the healing potential of play therapy and its ability to promote meaningful connections and boost emotional well-being and self-expression. This book provides information you can apply in your relationship with children as a parent, caregiver, or healthcare professional.

This book sets you on the path to enjoying a wonderful relationship with your children or those under your care. It is designed to help you understand and imbibe the strategies and techniques to harness the power of play to connect with your child's feelings and emotions.

This book will give you value not just for money but also for your *time investment.* You shouldn't hesitate to read this book, and you should begin now because you're in for a journey to discovering the power of play therapy!

Chapter 1: Introduction to Play Therapy

The mental health of every individual, children and adults alike, is crucial to the well-being and effectiveness of a person. Every day, in pursuit of happiness, people look for ways, sometimes new ones, to express themselves safely and comfortably. They also look for ways to forget about life's difficulties and experience peace and happiness.

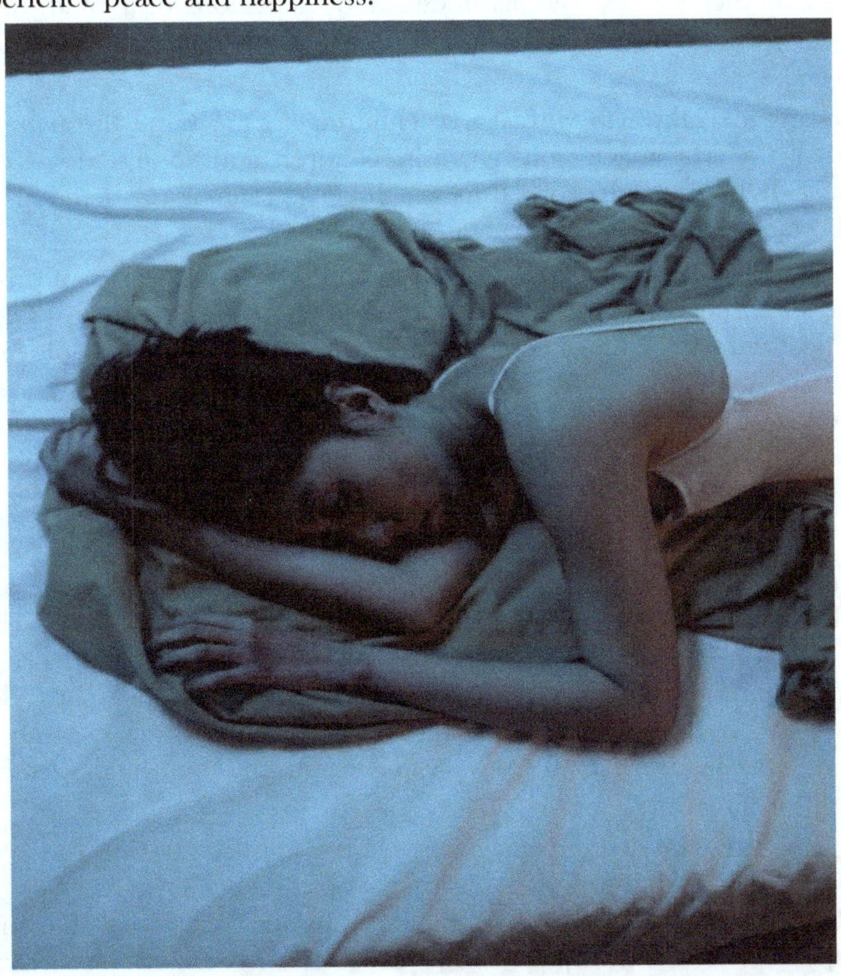

Mental health is a very crucial topic that cannot be ignored.
https://www.pexels.com/photo/a-woman-in-white-tank-top-lying-on-bed-6754068/

Everyone has different techniques that they favor. For some, it is sports, while for others, music, talking, and sharing their experiences with friends, but for children, the most comfortable form of expressing themselves and navigating their way to happiness is through play, which leads to the topic, "play therapy."

What Is Play Therapy?

Play therapy is a type of psychotherapy or counseling focusing mainly on children's mental healing and growth. This form of psychotherapy allows children to use play as a form of expression, given that they may not be able to fully articulate their feelings, thoughts, and emotions. Play therapy can be used on children aged 3-18, where materials, toys, and art are available for children to express themselves. In a conducive, attractive, and enabling environment, children feel safe and use play to communicate their thoughts to the play therapist.

Play therapy consists of methods that capitalize on children's natural urge to express themselves while also harnessing it to respond to and meet their developmental and mental needs. Children are very intelligent, and they quickly discover and learn new ways of coping with various experiences and dealing with things. Play therapy helps adults understand the actions of a child, the reasons for such actions, and how to help children cope in the face of difficulties without them having to verbally explain them.

While adults achieve that through verbalizing, children do the same through play. While adults communicate most of their feelings through words, children and young adolescents can achieve it through play therapy. It helps them work through difficulties, explore their feelings, and be more confident and comfortable.

The effectiveness of play therapy makes specialists apply it extensively as a means of intervention to complement a child's interpersonal and personal development. Play therapy isn't directed by anyone; children need certified mental health professionals like psychiatrists and psychologists. Social workers, behavioral occupational, and physical therapists can also handle play therapy sessions. Specialized programs are also carried out to educate and train mental health professionals on play therapy techniques.

Brief Overview of Play Therapy

Play therapy started originally as a theoretical model using systematic models to train professionals to understand and effectively communicate with children's feelings, but it is now a widely used form of psychotherapy. As a field of psychotherapy, play therapy's early ideas and theories have undergone redefining and transforming from theoretical knowledge to practical approaches. Some of its earliest methods and theories are no longer acceptable due to current ethics and research, but they played a huge role in advancing the field of play therapy. Some significant contributors to the development of the therapy include:

Hermine Hug-Hellmuth: The first recognized psychotherapist in the world to specialize in treating children was Hermine Hug-Hellmuth. She is regarded as having been the first person to use play as a type of therapy. By providing the kids in her care with the playthings they needed to express themselves, she helped to create formal play therapy in 1921. She went on to recommend utilizing play to examine kids.

David Levy: In 1938, he created a therapeutic approach named "release therapy."

Release therapy was a methodical, controlled strategy that helped traumatized kids engage in unstructured play. The therapist gradually introduced items related to the traumatic event, allowing kids to experience it again and express any unresolved acts or feelings.

Melanie Klein: Klein tried to get the attention of the kids she worked with in therapy by using play as an analytical tool. She thought that play gave access to a child's psyche.

Anna Freud: She provided several theoretical justifications for the idea that utilizing play as a form of therapy aids in developing a good rapport between the therapist and the child, granting the therapist greater access to the inner feelings and thoughts of the kid. She thought that play in children and free interaction in adults were fundamentally the same.

Carl Rogers: Carl Rogers invented person-centered therapy in the 1940s and 1950s. His approach to therapy placed a strong emphasis on the value of sincerity, acceptance, and trust in any therapeutic partnership.

Virginia Axline: By studying Rogers' person-centered therapy and modifying it to a play therapy technique more suitable for a child, she developed her nondirective play therapy.

Joseph Soloman: He developed an "active play" approach to help children who tended to act out impulsively. This strategy was founded purely on Soloman's conviction that a child's play-based expression of anger and terror will lead to more socially acceptable behavior.

Roger Phillips: Roger Phillips proposed the idea of integrating play therapy and cognitive therapy in the early 1980s as part of a more robust strategy to boost play therapy's efficacy. His theory has led to the application of cognitive behavioral play therapy in treating toddlers.

These key figures contributed immensely to developing play therapy into a therapeutic approach. Acting on these early concepts, research has extensively expounded on further possibilities play therapy can achieve.

Theories That Shape the Practice of Play Therapy

Play therapy has been significantly modified throughout history. Many theories have proven to be useful and effective and, thus, can be applied to help improve your child's well-being. Here are theories that have shaped the practice of play therapy:

Child-Centered Play Therapy

Like other play theories, child-centered play therapy acknowledges that play is an appropriate language when treating children. When properly engaged, play therapy can help children open up and interact more with their environment.

Cognitive Behavioral Play Therapy

It is a combination of cognitive therapy and play therapy, involving a range of cognitive behavioral approaches set to deactivate and dislodge inadequate phobias and social behaviors attributed to dysfunctional thoughts with the aim of replacing them with better thoughts. Cognitive behavioral play therapy tests the problem-solving capacity of the child, teaches alternative coping strategies, and tries to improve the emotional understanding and awareness of the child.

Family Play Therapy

The theory of family play therapy has long been in place and has helped families deal with their emotions rather than the child alone. It was designed to address and support the well-being of the entire family and the child while helping to redefine and reposition the family from where it currently is to where it can be.

Psychodynamic Play Therapy

It sees play as a medium to increase the child's level of developmental functionality. This theory of therapy proposes that there's more than one reason for behavior than what's observable. It uses play to examine children's feelings, opening the doors to understanding specific behavioral problems and exposing certain underlying issues. These theories have helped create approaches to gain easy access to a child's emotions and thoughts, help the child communicate them while feeling comfortable, and serve as a means to teach them coping skills to deal with their emotions. Some of such techniques include:

- Using building blocks
- Storytelling
- Sand and water play
- Board games
- Tea party play
- Play with dolls
- Dance and creative movement
- Strategy games like chess or checkers
- Puppet play
- Hide-and-seek
- Creative visualization
- Role-playing
- Reading
- Toy phones
- Card games
- Arts and crafts
- Musical play

These are some of the most common techniques play therapists use to promote healing and growth in children. A doll or puppet can help study the child's thinking and change their perspective about things. The therapist telling them to dress it up or look after it allows the child to form an attachment to the puppet, giving the child a sense of responsibility. In this way, a child's reaction to a stressful situation or responsibility can be observed.

Painting can also give insight into the child's creative abilities and mind. Some children may be able to paint out their feelings, providing the therapist an idea of their state of mind. Art therapy is very effective, and it can also help the child feel relaxed and less agitated and learn about acceptance when the child realizes that no matter the outcome of their painting, there's beauty in it.

Sand play or sand tray therapy helps a lot with visualization. While using miniature toys on the sand, the child can help visualize animals, people, and even situations. The scene created may reflect the child's life, giving them a chance to reflect, observe, resolve conflicts, make decisions, and gain self-acceptance. Some of these techniques may take a direct approach, others may not, but they are aimed at helping the child learn about their feelings and cope with them. The child can learn to tolerate others and become a more resilient and stronger version of themselves.

Benefits of Play Therapy for Children

Children don't have the verbal and cognitive skills to deal with very difficult experiences. For example, losing a loved one is hard for a child to process or even talk about, and they may use their toys or stuffed animals to represent the lost loved one. Play comes naturally as a way for them to express themselves. It helps them act out scenes, relax when stressed, or represent someone they love.

Play therapy helps children resolve conflicts, mirror their feelings, and learn coping strategies for their emotions. Many parents may not have heard of play therapy or may have been dismissive of it. However, it is a very effective and comfortable method to help children deal with their feelings. Some of the benefits of play therapy for children are:

- It helps the child to feel comfortable. Play therapy sessions help create an environment for the child to feel safe, comfortable, and supported.
- It helps children deal with stress and trauma-related events. Natural disasters, hospitalization, and relocation will affect a child's psyche. They may not have the skills to explain such feelings and may dismiss them. Still, through play therapy, they can express themselves using techniques tailored to help them relive such events and deal with the emotions related to them.
- Apart from dealing with stress and trauma-related events, it helps children overcome issues and problems related to those events. Play therapy helps children manage grief, loss, depression, social issues, anger, divorce of parents, trauma, aggression, school-related events, and physical and learning disabilities.
- It helps children cultivate social and communication skills over time.
- It helps them to be more responsible, especially for their actions. Play therapy sessions instill a sense of responsibility in a child.
- They're able to develop empathy and respect for themselves and others.

Roles of a Play Therapist in Therapeutic Process

A play therapist is a skilled and trained professional who works with children (and their families) to overcome difficult experiences and situations like anxiety, depression, death, family issues, neglect, traumatic experiences, or psychological issues. The play therapist uses play to understand the actions and reactions of the child while communicating with the child's family to gain an encompassing knowledge of the situation.

The play therapist possesses the following traits:

- Emotional resilience
- Excellent communication skills
- Knowledge of psychology
- Good physical fitness
- A friendly, patient countenance

- Understanding and sensitivity

These characteristics are necessary to help the therapist manage children's strong, resilient will. Good physical shape is needed to help the therapist participate in activities with the child. The therapist also undergoes training to get certified and licensed before working with children. The therapist needs a psychology, occupational therapy, mental health nursing, or early childhood studies degree. Before commencing work as a play therapist, the therapist must also have experience working with children in schools, hospitals, or any capacity and certification from the Association of Play Therapists.

Play therapists help children access and overcome feelings they never thought they would. The therapist builds a strong relationship, making them feel safe and comfortable in their presence. The therapist uses various techniques while working with parents to ensure the child moves past troubling experiences and starts feeling comfortable and secure again. Play therapists can work with schools and childcare centers to help tackle issues affecting a child's growth and interpersonal development.

Limitations and Challenges of Play Therapy

While play therapy is very effective and helps the therapist and parents reach the child's inner thoughts and feelings, play therapy is still subject to challenges. The therapist faces the bulk of these challenges, and if not properly handled, this can affect the child, family, and the relationship between the child and therapist. Here are 4 challenges associated with play therapy:

1. Expectations of Parents and Adults

Parents care for their children, and in doing so, they bring them to a play therapist after realizing that something isn't right with the child. Before beginning therapy sessions, the therapist is briefed (necessarily) on the history of the child, the problems, and the context. The therapist will sometimes encounter the problem of reconciling the parents' expectations and the need to allow the child to express themselves freely. Working to meet both demands is sometimes challenging and puts strain on the process of communicating effectively with the child.

2. Deciding the Type of Play Therapy and Materials to Use

Play therapists are responsible for deciding what creative materials or toys to place in their office while keeping the child's interests and passions at heart. The type of play therapy to use, which will affect the outcome of the therapy and relationship with the child, is based on the knowledge of the play therapist.

3. Need for Specialized Programs

The extent of knowledge a play therapist has will reflect in the quality of the sessions. Play therapists without proper training and experience in childcare can be limited in the resources they use to produce results from therapy sessions.

4. Collaborating with Other Professionals

Sometimes, play therapists must work with other professionals like psychiatrists, guidance counselors, and social workers to broaden their knowledge of childcare and their clients. Lack of experience in the area of childcare is a setback for those who aim to become play therapists. Relevant experience in working with children is a non-negotiable requirement for becoming a play therapist.

Play therapy is a form of psychotherapy that deals with the issues and difficulties a child faces in their personal and interpersonal development. It encompasses a host of methods and techniques aimed at helping children connect with their inner thoughts and feelings while overcoming stress and trauma-related issues and events, as well as learning coping mechanisms. Key figures like Anna Freud, Carl Rogers, and Hermine Hug-Hellmuth, amongst others, carved the theories and techniques that shaped this practice over time, and it became increasingly refined on its way to becoming established as a therapeutic approach.

Play to children is what verbalization is to adults. Play creates energy and is a form of expression for children in their developmental stages. Play therapy is a way to show more care to children, especially those who don't deal easily with their emotions. Parents can shower more love and attention on their children by collaborating with the play therapist to get in tune with their emotions. Play therapy is not just an opportunity for the child to learn and deal with emotions but also to heal and grow.

Chapter 2: Developmental Play Therapy

Play is a child's love language; it always gets them high-spirited, and they enjoy the fun moments that come with it. Besides the fun it brings, it broadens your child's knowledge and how they express themselves. It frees them from stress and loneliness, connecting them to things and the people around them. These benefits cannot be over-emphasized. They can explore a lot of creativity, and many of their emotions can be kept in check. This is a stage a child must go through for them to understand themselves and the world better. It is a part of their development.

Playing with your children allows them to be comfortable to express themselves around you as it develops your relationship.
https://www.pexels.com/photo/cheerful-mother-and-daughter-having-fun-on-bed-at-home-3756036/

What is the effect on a child when they find it hard to express themselves emotionally or verbally? Or what happens when they've reached the age when they adopt certain characteristics of their peers? How do you know when your child has unusual stress levels or challenges when socializing with those around them? As an adult, you can relate to having faced some emotional, mental, or even social difficulties, which led you to share your thoughts or feelings with someone who could counsel or help you. This isn't always so for children. They are young and vibrant, yet they may not have enough vocabulary to pinpoint what might be wrong with them at certain times. And that is where Play Therapy helps.

In this chapter, you'll be shown how play therapy can support your child's development at every growth stage. You'd also be given a heads-up about what you should expect if your child ever struggles with developmental challenges and how play therapy can be specifically applied at such times.

How Play Therapy Enhances Children's Development

Play therapy is used mainly for children from ages 3-18 years. These children and adolescents need a space in their lives where they can feel comfortable expressing themselves. Imagine a room with toys and play aids (dolls, puppets, stuffed animals, Lego, etc.). Your child can pick anything from craft materials, crayons, pencils, and drawing sheets. All these materials help them express how they feel about you or themselves at any given time. When children think they're free to explore this space however they want, doing any activity they like, it improves how they express themselves. This is the core purpose of play therapy in your child's development.

What, then, are those developmental challenges children are likely to encounter?

- Communication or speech
- Motor skills
- Social interactions
- Problem-solving

Every challenge here is only based on comparison with children of the same age. The developmental challenge determines a child's need for therapy, and therapy should only be administered based on his/her needs and preferences. Instead of the treatment being limited, giving children the freedom to choose their own means of expressing themselves, a wide variety of treatment choices is more effective, leading to a far better chance of healing. In other words, allow the child to choose his/her method of communication. It also builds a relationship between the child and the therapist. Remember, the role of a therapist is not to condemn or exaggerate the underlying issue. Instead, it is to reflect on what they find and create a way out of it. The first and most important thing is to *build trust with the child.*

According to Lucy Bowen, Executive Dir. National Association for Play Therapy, India:

> *"A child's healing process or challenge resolution is far more important than the therapist's interpretation of the play. Through this play and with great assistance from therapists, children may now be able to better interpret those confusing feelings and understand themselves and the world around them."*

Development in Children

A child's development can be improved with the right kind of practice at home in conjunction with therapeutic sessions. However, this doesn't mean that children are unlikely to do well without therapy, as many grow perfectly well without therapeutic attention. But for kids with developmental challenges or a traumatic past, autistic challenges, and the like, close attention and therapy are required. Apart from this, take a look at the normal course of child development:

Development in a child may refer to sequential growth in physical appearance, language, communication, thought patterns, and emotional changes. When this happens, they become more independent of guidance and assistance from their parent or guardian. They begin to do certain tasks by themselves. For example, when infants learn to walk, they will no longer need their parents to help teach them to take these steps.

Some hereditary genetic expressions can greatly influence their development. That is one of many factors. Their development is also affected by their environment and the pace at which they learn or take in information. As discussed, development can be in cognitive abilities, speech progress, social interaction, physical and emotional growth, etc. To overcome any challenge your child may encounter while growing up, gaps between their abilities and those of other children their age must be minimized. Confidence and frustration levels also need to be managed.

Play Therapy in the World of a Child's Development

Play therapy is very effective for children struggling with communication and emotional imbalance, especially those suffering from psychological, mental, or social health challenges. It generates a coping mechanism for stress, anger, anxiety, sadness, and neglect. It is also effective for children with delayed development, autism, and ADHD. Since children may find it hard to regulate their emotions compared to adults, this method gives them room for expression. Challenges in child development can arise from physical, mental, or even sexual abuse. Sometimes, a child is abandoned and suffers neglect from the people who are supposed to protect them, or they may even have had to witness violence or have been victims.

At a very young age, they have limited means of communication and may find it difficult or almost impossible to explain or describe events. This may be due to fear, pain, or even shame. On the occasion where, despite the odds, they still want to talk, they may struggle due to limited communication skills. When these kids lack a way to express their feelings, they direct them through other means. It could be anger, tears, harming themselves, anxiety, harming others, or mental isolation. But with play therapy, children get to have fun while dealing with their issues, which helps them express themselves. Play therapy also helps children learn to keep their emotions in check.

Common Developmental Challenges in Children

A delay in a child's development may mean they have not yet reached the milestone expected for their age group. Delay may be in their speech, hearing ability, motor function, or vision. It's different and understandable if a child is premature, but as they grow, if the delays are persistent, it usually indicates that the child needs a check-up. However, don't panic unnecessarily; never forget that each child develops at their own pace.

Here are some common developmental challenges in a child:

- **Disorder in Receptiveness**

This disorder is the first speech development problem a child may display. Here, the child cannot identify shapes, colors, and other forms of objects or body parts. Although they can be taught, getting them to learn will take some time. As these kids grow older, you must have a well-thought-out plan ahead for them to address this disorder, even if it means seeing a pediatrician.

- **Disorder in Expressive Language**

This is quite common in children while growing up. It's the inability to verbalize large expressive words or sentences. Occasionally, they will pronounce short and brief words like "Ma, Bah! Nah!" but that's it. As they get older, this may be a challenge. You will need to work with a specialist to address this challenge.

- **Motor Delays**

Here, a parent may notice that their child is making very slow progress in learning to walk or even hold things with their hands. They may also be unable to brush their teeth or do basic things children in their age group can do. You must deal with this particular challenge as soon as possible so they do not get used to being assisted and become overly dependent.

- **Cognitive Delay**

Cognitive delays can play out in different ways. Some kids may experience slow speech production, while some struggle to understand simple concepts. All these delays will make it hard for them to keep up with their peers in school.

Stages of a Child's Development and Play Therapy Techniques to Apply

As a child crosses into adolescence, they have grown in physical appearance, speech development, and intellect. With these changes, you can easily track your child's growth to know when there is a disorder or delay in development. There are several categories to classify a child's growth, as proposed by different experts. Some experts have classified them into six, some four, and others five. The major changes are observed at specific ages even while the number of this classification differs. With each developmental stage comes the need to also apply specific approaches using play therapy techniques. Adolescence cannot be approached using toys or crayons as that is more suitable for toddlers. Here are five different stages of a child's growth and techniques you can apply that have proven very effective for a child at any stage:

1. Newborns

From zero to three months, babies can respond to external stimuli. That means they can follow the direction of sounds with their heads, grin at you, and make movements with their hands while crying to indicate that they're hungry or need a nap. Helpful techniques to apply include:

- Making gestures with the face
- Singing
- Cuddling

2. Infants

Babies here are aged between 3-12 months old. They start to display new abilities when they get to this stage. At 3-6 months, they have more control of their hands and legs and can wiggle them back and forth. They also begin to recognize faces and babble. From 6-8 months, they can now sit without much support. They can also respond when people call them by name, make gestures, clap hands, and pick up little objects. From 9-12 months, they begin to crawl and even hold stuff for support when they want to stand. They can also mimic certain sounds and gestures. Consider these play techniques:

- Singing
- Cuddling

- Tickling
- Dancing in costumes or the peek-a-boo method

3. Toddler

Toddlers are children from ages 1-3 years old. At this stage, they know how to walk without support. They can make short runs and even climb furniture. They can also hold crayons and pencils, wave, and say short words and sentences. Here are some helpful techniques:

- Playing hide and seek
- Using stuffed bunnies or animals to demonstrate activities and emotions while telling stories.
- Playing interactive games with them
- Playing characters with customs to tell stories

4. Preschool

Preschool ranges from ages 3-5 years. They can now throw and catch things at lengthy distances and hop and jump easily. They can brush their teeth and even dress themselves to some extent. They are now able to pronounce words completely and speak relatively clearly. They can draw and trace words with a pencil and a little assistance. By four and above, they can bathe or use the bathroom alone. You can try giving them the means to express themselves on their own. Here are some helpful ways:

- Practicing drawing or painting
- Playing in the sand
- Playing with toys and puppets
- Graphic storytelling with guided images

5. Adolescence/School Age

By now, kids will be between 6-18 years old. At this stage, children live in complete dependence on themselves. They have their own opinions and want to be heard. They begin to speak more fluently, write more clearly, and behave more decently. They express some emotions like love, anger, sadness, and envy through words, thoughts, and sometimes actions. They start to form a community, making (and being) friends. When they get to puberty (11-17 years), they develop sexually. To make your child come out of their shells, try out these helpful techniques:

- Group discussions
- Theatre arts
- Engage in collaborative problem-solving activities
- Dance drama
- Art therapy, and so on.

Using the techniques above, you can measure (or trace) the pace at which your child develops. If your child is lagging behind in any way, make sure to book an appointment with a therapist or pediatrician. A pediatrician will run a diagnostic test and tell you if your child needs further treatment. Be aware that some children develop slower than others.

People of different age groups can adopt play therapy, but in this chapter, you learn how it is applied specifically to children and adolescents. They are very helpful techniques therapists use to get children to come out of their shells. To close the communication gap between you as an adult and a child, you must have learned that children have limited communication expressive skills. Therefore, you must create a world where they feel safe, free, and comfortable to express themselves.

With every stage of development, infancy, toddlers, preschool, and adolescence, there are certain characteristics they should portray. You could be dealing with a disorder or slow growth if these milestones are not evident. Either way, seeing a pediatrician or a therapist for professional help would be wise. You're a child's first hope for change, so make sure you lead and help them when needed.

Chapter 3: The Parent-Child Connection

There's no doubt that being a parent is really fulfilling. However, this job doesn't come without its challenges. Managing a family as a modern parent is not easy at all, and with the numerous burdens on both parental figures, it's hard to enforce a strong parent-child connection. Although parents want what's best for their kids, they struggle to manage a deep relationship with them while dealing with work, household activities, and societal pressures. Yet, there's nothing better you can give your children than love, affection, and attention. Kids are known to learn and develop best when they have strong, loving, and positive relationships with their parents and caregivers.

Building a connection with your children is vital.

https://www.pexels.com/photo/happy-mother-and-children-hugging-at-home-4474043/

For many people, being parents and connecting with their kids comes naturally, but it's not as simple for many others. The latter usually happens with people who didn't get much love, affection, and value during childhood. However, the good news is that parenting skills can be quickly learned. So, this chapter will explain how essential a strong parent-child connection is for your kids and what you can do to build a secure relationship with your child, whether they're toddlers, elementary students, tweens, or teens.

Why Building a Secure Relationship with Your Child Matters

There's no other relationship like the one between a parent and their child. This relationship is solely responsible for a child's emotional, physical, and social development. And there's no such thing as giving your child too much love. In fact, the more love and nurturing you provide them with, the better for their well-being. The kind of connection you have with your child may not affect you that much, but it definitely lays the foundation for your child's personality, how they behave, and even the life choices they make when they are older. It is so crucial that you build a good relationship with your child, not for just your sake, but for theirs, because:

- The chances of children forming stable relationships with others are higher if they grow up with a secure, healthy, happy, and consistent attachment to their parents.
- Children who have good relationships with their parents can regulate their emotions much better when compared to those who come from abusive or detached parents.
- A strong emotional bond between parents and children enhances their mental, linguistic, and emotional abilities.
- This bond between parent and child also plays a crucial role when fostering healthy and confident social behaviors in the child.
- Smaller children and teens with healthy relationships with their parents have higher self-esteem than those without. They're also capable of forming genuine friendships with their peers.

Ensuring that your child gets the love and affection they deserve from you is a prerequisite for healthy brain development and social upbringing. There's nothing wrong with treating your children with the love and respect they deserve. This is not the equivalent of spoiling your child. Spoiling means giving in to their every whim, whereas being loving and affectionate means you treat your children with the warmth and respect they need. When you notice your child's needs and respond to them lovingly, your little one will feel more at ease. Whether you're dealing with a newborn, toddler, or adolescent, you must treat them with all the love you can muster, even if you come from a family that wasn't very affectionate toward you.

Barriers to a Strong Parent-Child Connection

It's long been established that for a child to become resilient, a strong parent-child connection is necessary starting from a young age. But a parent-child connection is not just about being loving and affectionate with your child. It's also about setting boundaries and making them feel seen and heard. The key behaviors that account for this type of connection are not taught to parents, so most of them struggle with this relationship. There are some other problems when it comes to creating a strong parent-child relationship, including:

- Parents are often advised to ignore a crying child to build their resilience, making parents believe that children are manipulative rather than simply unskilled at meeting their needs. This makes you unable to connect fully with your child and form a strong parent-child relationship.
- Parental stress and anxiety make it even harder for parents to be emotionally skilled.
- Every parent has made the mistake of being harsh or not understanding towards their children when they're stressed.
- The competing demands on a parent's time make it very challenging to give their children the time and attention they deserve, particularly when their child is undergoing sensitive developmental changes.

All of this results in a weaker understanding between the parents and their children.

Play Therapy Techniques

Play therapy has proven effective in establishing a strong bond between a parent and a child. It helps you engage in play alongside your child and create a safe space for them where they can freely share their feelings and thoughts. Most children are hesitant or unable to communicate their thoughts through words, so play therapy is an excellent way to get them out of their shells and help parents grow closer to them. This shared playtime builds trust, empathy, and understanding, allowing you to connect more deeply. Play therapy is a chance to have fun, grow closer, and create lasting memories with your children.

Family Play Therapy

Family play therapy can be particularly effective for improving communication and connection between family members. These activities need the whole family to participate:

- **Memory Capsule (Any Age)**

A memory capsule game is perfect for some good quality family time and for reminiscing about family memories. The best part is that this activity is suitable for children of all ages, starting from 4 or 5, and even including your teens.

MEMORY CAPSULE
MY TIME CAPSULE
THE YEAR IS
IM
YEARS OLD
My Favorite movie:
My Favorite book:
My Favorite song:
My Favorite hobby:
My Favorite game:
My Favorite color:
MY FAMILY:
Things to include in time capsule:
- Photos
- Drawings
- Crafts
- Newspaper and
magazine clippings
- list of goals or thoughts
about future
- Drawings
- Hand/paw prints
- Ticket stubs

Here are the instructions you should follow:

Materials:

- A container (e.g., a shoebox or a jar) to serve as the memory capsule
- Art supplies (colored pencils, markers, stickers, etc.)
- Paper or small notecards
- Scissors
- Glue or tape
- Meaningful items or mementos (photographs, concert tickets, seashells, letters, etc.)

Instructions:

- Gather all the necessary materials for the activity, and explain to your child what this activity is about.
- Ask each family member to offer one memento or meaningful item and share the story behind it. For instance, this could be from a family trip, a milestone event, or something simple.
- Encourage your child to share their story and how it makes them feel.
- These items can be anything that holds significance to your family, such as photographs, concert tickets, seashells, letters, drawings, or even small trinkets.
- Cut up small pieces of paper to act as labels. Add names and short stories for each memento.
- Once you place everything in the memory capsule, you can ask your child to decorate the container using art supplies, stickers, or paint. Encourage them to be creative.
- They can write their names or draw a family picture on the memory capsule.
- Find a safe place to store the container; it could be in the attic storage or even buried in your garden.
- After a few months or even years, get that memory capsule out of its hiding place and reminisce about your memories together.

Cooperative Games

Parents and caregivers have used cooperative games for many years. These usually exist as multi-player board games in which the players must work together as a team to complete a challenge. The kids have to share ideas, make group decisions, and practice problem-solving to reach a common goal. Unlike non-competitive games that focus on enjoyment, cooperative board games target the idea of competing, not against each other but rather against the game. This teaches children teamwork, communication, and problem-solving. Here are some board games you can try:

1. Caves and Claws (Ages 6 and up)

This game is for fantasy adventure enthusiasts and can be played by two to four people. In the game sequence, the players have to work as a team of archeologists who venture into a jungle to look for ancient artifacts. They have to overcome challenges, create paths, and search for treasure while working to stay alive.

2. Lord of the Rings (Ages 12 and up)

If you or your child is a LOTR fan, this game is perfect for your bonding time! This board game needs a minimum of two players but can be extended to five players as well. Ask the children to take on the role of the hobbits and work together to destroy the One Ring. It's a super fun game to play with your tweens and teens.

3. Save the Whales (Ages 8 and up)

This game is designed for two to four players, where the players have to work together to beat evil forces like oil spills or catcher ships that endanger the lives of the great whales. You can win the game by eliminating all dangers and saving the eight whales.

Playful Storytelling

Children are known for keeping many of their thoughts, feelings, and problems to themselves instead of communicating them to adults or even their friends. It doesn't matter whether they are scared to share their feelings or not consciously aware of what is bothering them. What matters is that they have difficulty communicating and releasing their emotions. Even if you ask them several times what's wrong, their answer may be "*Nothing*" or *"I don't know."* This is where playful storytelling techniques come in. This method of communication will help your child creatively express their emotions. This particular method, known as the garbage method, is designed to help children release problems they're holding on to and then follow up by playing out these problems to find a solution.

Materials Needed

- Two brown sandwich bags
- Colored pencils or markers
- Twelve strips of paper to write problems on

Process (Ages 4 to 8)

Begin the process by handing the child one paper bag and asking them to draw on it. Take the second bag and take part in the drawing activity yourself. While you're both drawing, ask your child about "garbage" in a friendly manner, like this:

> *"Do you know what garbage is? It's the dirty stuff you put in the garbage can when there's no use for it. But what if no one picked up all the garbage we threw out? What if weeks and months of garbage were left in our home? Then, there wouldn't be any space to sit, eat or sleep. We'd never get rid of the garbage. Well, we keep garbage in ourselves as well. These are things that bother us, things that give us a yucky feeling. So, let's finish our drawings, and then I will give you six pieces of paper on which you can write the garbage you're keeping inside you, and then we will throw this garbage in our garbage bags."*

Start by writing down a problem you assume your child has to show them how to start putting their own garbage down on paper. Ask them to write any feelings, problems, etc., that they feel at home, in school, outside, with friends, with their siblings, etc. Once you've done that, place these pieces of paper into the garbage bag and close it. Take a break, and then role-play the problems your child is having, and help them come up with a suitable solution. Maybe your child is scared of the dark. Validate their feelings, never mock their problems, and explain to your child that it's okay to feel this way. Then, provide them with a few solutions like "*Maybe you could have a nightlight in your room?*"

Theraplay

This method involves a series of games and activities that promote bonding, communication, and social interaction. This game involves rolling the dice with different communication prompts or topics written on each side and engaging in discussions based on the prompt that appears facing upwards.

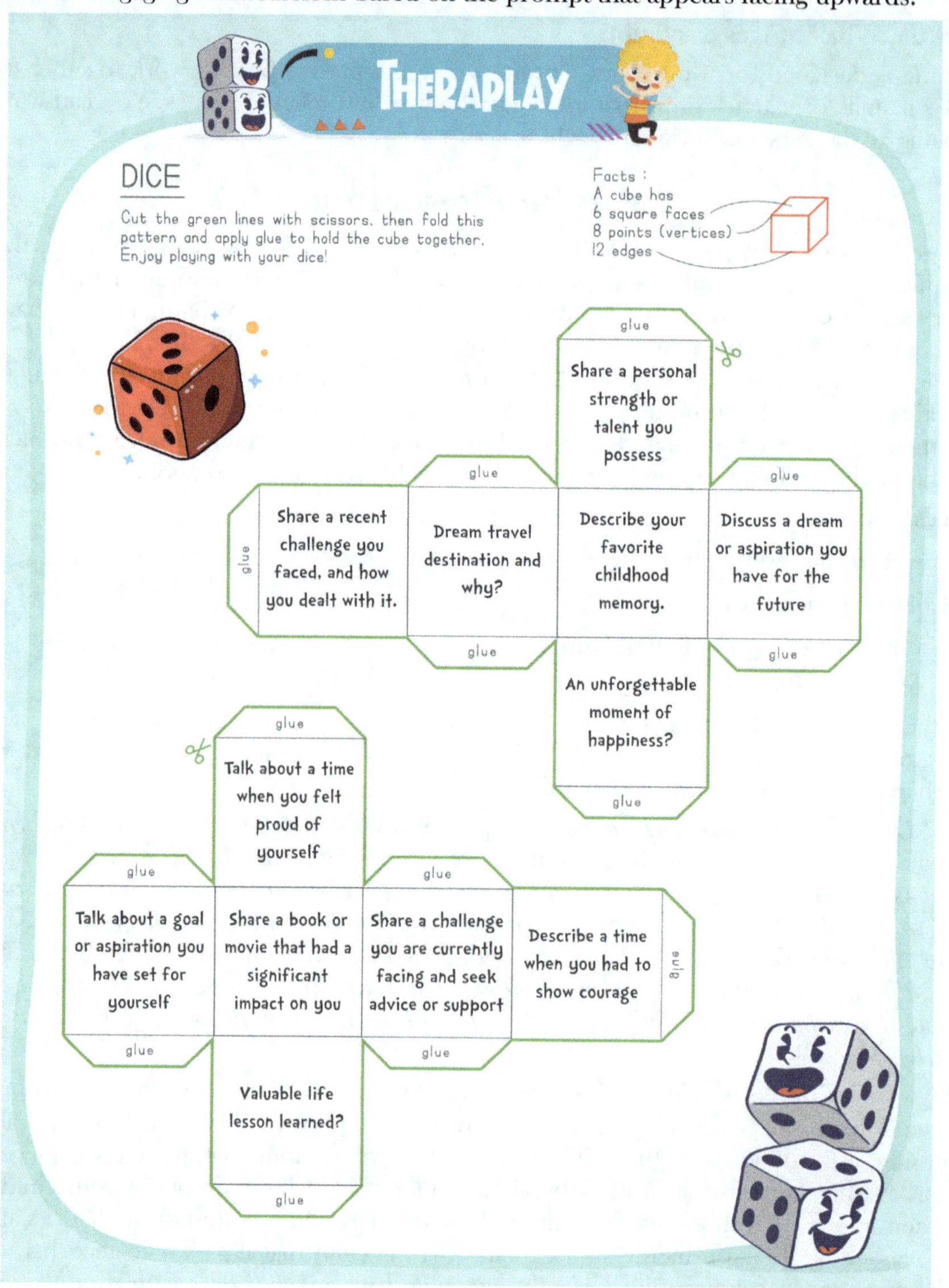

Materials Needed:

- Printable dice template
- Printer and paper
- Scissors or craft knife
- Adhesive (glue, tape, or stickers)
- Optional: Cardstock or laminating sheets for durability

Instructions:

1. Print, fold, and glue together the two printable dice given below.
2. You can paste the dice template onto cardstock for added durability.
3. The game needs at least two players, but it is more fun when played in a group.
4. Sit in a circle on the ground or at a table and take turns rolling the dice.
5. Read the prompt out loud and share your thoughts on the topic. This will set an example for your child, and they won't be as hesitant to participate.
6. Make sure you create a comfortable and non-judgmental space where your children can freely express themselves.

Setting Boundaries

For most parents, setting boundaries for their children is second nature. "Don't hit," "Don't interrupt." "Don't fight." However, as children grow, setting social boundaries for them is equally important. Making your children learn how to set boundaries is also equally essential. It helps to start early. When you teach your children to talk about their feelings and emotions at a young age, they are more likely to understand the concept of boundaries. For example, you can ask your child:

"*How do you think Amy felt when you took her toy away?*"

or

"*How do you feel when your sister won't let you play with her friends?*"

While you should teach your children to be empathetic, you should also teach them how to stand up for themselves when their peers are being pushy.

The parent-child connection is an irreplaceable bond that shapes the lives of both parties involved. Through this unique relationship, children learn to love, trust, and be resilient. Nurturing this connection requires open communication, empathy, and active engagement. As parents, you must recognize your presence and support's profound impact on your children's emotional well-being and development.

Chapter 4: Developing Social Skills through Play

Playing is the truest way to allow children (from the youngest age to adolescence) to release their energy, build character, and learn life skills.

Using play to develop social skills is a technique that was used long before any studies were made. If anyone in history wanted their children to have a healthy social group to rely on, they sent them out at a young age to find other kids their age to play with and bond with.

Having social skills is not always easy. As people grow up, they learn how to maintain relationships. Sometimes, you need to implement well-thought-out strategies or ways to resolve conflict. Whether it's learning how to settle arguments so you can reach a middle ground or trying to see things from the perspective of others, all of these skills are methods used to sustain healthy connections.

Play Therapy's Effect on Social Skills

When engaging with new groups, children learn through others' and shared experiences. They are allowed to articulate their emotions, explore their feelings, learn discipline, and work out the challenges that life usually throws at them.

Using play therapy in a safe and contained environment allows a child to understand the social norms of society without being subjected to unpredictable consequences. It gives them a safe space to express their feelings and removes destructive social dynamics they could experience in other situations and relationships. In other words, it's a safe place for learning.

For example, suppose a child in a contained setting with a therapist starts to lose control of their emotions and screams. In that case, the therapist will start adapting gentle techniques to allow the child to understand the social cues of the real world, like saying, "Use the inside voice when inside." They could also do something as simple as asking questions, asking the child to tell a story with puppets, and then engaging in conversations with the characters they create.

These methods allow the child to understand boundaries and implement the correct behavior to its corresponding situation, allowing the child to understand the expectations of every social setting. They learn when to contain their emotions and when to express them. They also encourage cooperation and problem-solving.

Impact on Children with ADHD

According to an Australian study back in 2016, children with ADHD benefit greatly from play therapy by learning to make and keep friends.

Children suffering from ADHD exhibit impulsivity, not playing nice with others, hyperactivity, and difficulty taking turns. As they usually have trouble translating social cues, especially at a young age, this could cause negative effects, which could be carried further into their lives as they grow older.

Three universities (Curtin University in Perth, the University of Sydney, and Australian Catholic University) were involved in testing these theories and the effectiveness of play therapy on ADHD children. The study was conducted on 29 children divided into two groups. One was subjected to play therapy for ten weeks, and the other was placed in a control group (who received play therapy after the 10-week period).

The ten-week therapy was divided into three parts: sessions with a professional therapist in charge of structured play, at-home follow-up programs parents needed to adhere to, and a weekly feedback session to report on the child's progress.

A test was designed to measure the effectiveness of the intervention program called the test of Playfulness (TOP). It was conducted at the beginning of the trial and at the end to measure the child's progress in terms of engagement, sharing, and comprehension of silent and spoken social cues.

As the study reached its end, there were significant improvements in the children's TOP scores, noting that the ones with the lowest scores at the beginning now had the greatest boost to their social skills.

Though the study was small, it had very promising results and provided hope that this type of therapy could be used on autistic children to enhance their social interactions.

Impact on Preschoolers

Play is crucial for developing long-term relationships and building trust at this particular stage in a child's life.

Play activates the imagination, encouraging creativity in children, and improves their communication skills in the first real-world environment where they encounter new people, develop their first impressions and perspectives of how relationships work, and work out techniques to create their own little circle of trustees.

In previous studies (Holis, 2017), it was deduced that role-play games have a significant impact on developing a child's social and emotional health.

They affect the child's learning by encouraging freedom of expression and moments of exploration, allowing the children to use what they learn in the make-believe game to act effectively in the face of an adversary.

Another set of games that have been effective for developing children's social skills has been group puzzles. They allow the child to engage with social norms such as waiting for their turn and cooperating to achieve a unified goal while at the same time impacting them mentally and emotionally.

In a 2012 study, Puteh and Ali reported that implementing play therapy to improve social skills may be less effective if the teacher/parents are not properly prepared or trained to use the methods correctly. It is necessary to encourage educators to be creative when implementing the methods and incorporating different types of activities to equally cover the child's physical, emotional, and social development.

Impact on Adolescence

Play therapy was applied as a resolution method to groups afflicted by the global lockdown that happened due to the COVID-19 virus.

This application allowed the patients to communicate more effectively with family members and enhanced their development and self-actualization.

The restrictions placed during the lockdown caused some young adults to become much more dependent upon their caregivers, making it a struggle to get back to the daily routine of school days and social interactions with their peers and teachers.

Being exposed to screens for extended periods as the only way to pass the time during confinement sometimes had negative effects that essentially led to psychosocial issues.

Both thirteen and fourteen-year-olds were included in this study.

Five sessions were conducted. These were ice-breaking sessions (sand play therapy), expressing emotions through expressive art therapy or using an emotional ball, communication skills sessions (finding common ground), self-care and care for others (puppets), and lastly, appreciating each other through a "you've got mail" game which encouraged the participants to write each other letters at the end of a session as an act of acceptance of themselves and others.

After all five sessions, each group member showed improvement in their social behavior. Classmates of members of the groups noted a change in their overall demeanors and attitudes. These members were able to get along with others, adapt and communicate more effectively than at the start of the study, and improve their adjustment techniques.

Types of Therapy

Most treatments using Play Therapy can be divided into two styles: Directive and Non-Directive.

Directive

You can probably work out the method from the name. This type of therapy depends upon directions delivered by the therapist during games.

The games are usually structured and goal-oriented, with the reins of the proceedings being in the therapist's hand, by which he/she controls the pace of the game and the exposure the child is getting.

Non-Directive

Based on research, this type of therapy has produced more positive outcomes than the directive approach. Children have a remarkable talent for achieving great heights on their own when given a chance while only provided with small triggers or tools without the hands-on supervision of a professional.

Symptoms of Difficulties in Play and Social Skills

If a child is having trouble engaging and adapting to social connections built through play, you may notice these behaviors:

- Upending toys on the ground
- Failure to recognize others' emotions and verbal/non-verbal cues
- Difficulty in maintaining friendships
- Constant interruptions
- Lack of concentration
- Narrow interest in toys and games
- No comprehension of consequences

Therapy Games and Activities

Now let's explore a list of games recommended to improve a child's social interactions and emotional balance which have given positive results;

1. Roll the Ball

This game is suitable for young children, such as toddlers and preschoolers.

It is a simple concept of rolling a ball between two children, using measured strength to get it to the other end without injuring their playmate.

This game helps them with the notion of taking turns in conversations or when performing other tasks. It also teaches self-control.

2. Legos (Individual and Group)

This is an accessible play activity for most children. Therapists usually divide it into easily attainable projects together with conversation topics. These types of games allow the child to implement a mix of creativity and engagement techniques in the real world.

3. Juggling thoughts

This game emphasizes being present and stops a child from being introspective.

The game is suitable for older children and adolescents.

1. Start the game by standing a group in a circle facing each other.
2. Start by passing objects to one group member and ask them to start circulating them.
3. Ask the group to increase the speed of the circulation.
4. Tell them to stop the movement and explain that the objects are to be imagined as thoughts.
5. Tell them to start again and move it quickly among them, then slow down.
6. Explain that being present and mindful slows down the intrusion of thoughts.
7. And then discuss how it felt for the thoughts to come in quickly versus when they slowed down.

4. The Name Game

This game is suitable for toddlers and young children. One of the fundamental lessons in social interactions is getting someone's attention and understanding their point of view.

1. Seat the children in a circle and hand one of them a ball.
2. Ask the child with the ball to select another child in the group, speak their name, and pass the ball to them.
3. The child who receives the ball should repeat the same task with someone else until all the names of participants have been spoken.

5. Staring Contest

A lot of younger children have trouble holding eye contact in a conversation.

This type of contest allows them to practice looking people in the eye. If the child, however, is still struggling, start small. Place a small sticker on your forehead and ask them to look at that instead while maintaining a conversation.

6. The Topic Game

There are several variations to this game. The most commonly used among teachers is choosing a topic -for example, animals – and asking the kids to name them alphabetically.

This exercise helps them focus on one subject and follow instructions until the job is done. It allows creativity when they get to the more challenging letters with limited options.

7. Emotion Charades

This game allows children to pick up on social cues and the nonverbal emotional reactions of others.

The game is similar to regular charades, with the slight difference that a child mimics an emotion, and the rest of the group needs to guess the emotion correctly.

8. Checker Stack

One of the challenges children face is keeping up with one conversation. This challenge is highlighted, particularly if the child has autism.

This game helps them stay on topic.

You'll need a stack of tokens, like poker chips, divided between two players. The first player will place a token and initiate a conversation. Then, the second contributor should respond with a statement relevant to the conversation that started and stack his or her token on top of his or her own prize pile. This continues until one of the children says something irrelevant, at which point the game is effectively over. You can then get the children to start another topic.

9. Community Gardening

This is a game for most ages. Gardening is a bit different, especially if performed within a group, as it enhances social skills and teaches responsibility by caring for a living environment or a particular plant.

It can also calm down any stress or nervousness through the use of focus on an outdoor task.

10. Productive Debate

This is more effective with older kids and adolescents. It allows the contestants a chance to show how emotionally intelligent they are and how positive they can be in challenging settings.

Those who can succeed in carrying out a debate without turning it into a fight are often more likely to have leadership roles in their lives.

11. Scavenger Hunts

This game, like its namesake, is quite simple and applicable for all ages. The goal is to allocate an object or solve riddles and problems to get a reward, all of which has to be done as a cooperative group split into pairs or more extensive groups of children.

They learn to be organized, work as a team, and make collective decisions. They also get rewarded for cooperating together.

12. Team Sports

Participation in these sports is usually through school or recreational teams or even through neighborhood friends. It emphasizes focus, working to achieve a common goal, and emotional recognition of when someone is hurt or loses the game.

13. Playing with Characters

Using dolls or stuffed animals encourages children to interact. Building conversations through toys, whether in a group or individually, allows them to express their emotions and practice social activities with imaginary friends through the toys.

Chapter 5: Expressing and Regulating Emotions

Everyone is born with emotions, but these emotions are not naturally pre-wired into your brain. Sure, babies are born with instinctive reactions like crying, frustration, hunger, and pain, but they come into contact with many other emotions as they grow. There are varied arguments about emotional development, with some people believing that emotions are built-in and discovered as you age, while others say that emotions are learned from social and cultural contexts. It is, however, widely accepted that there are eight natural primary emotions: anger, fear, sadness, joy, surprise, delight, curiosity, and embarrassment.

Frustration, sadness, and anger – leading to crying – are three of the most common emotions children show.
https://www.pexels.com/photo/boy-in-white-polo-shirt-crying-3905727/

These emotions are felt in different variations. Resentment and violence are different levels of anger, while anxiety is just another intensity of fear. All secondary emotions are linked to the eight fundamental emotions and reflect a person's emotional reactions to specific feelings or situations. Many argue that emotions are learned from the experiences a person has during their lifetime. Ergo, children are not very aware of their emotions and have a hard time managing them. They are constantly learning as they go.

Let's say a child was punished after a tantrum. The next time they get angry, they may start to feel anxious. Similarly, if a child is made fun of after expressing their fear, they will feel embarrassed the next time they get scared.

How you react to your child's emotions will greatly impact their emotional intelligence. When your kids feel emotionally invalidated, they're more likely to struggle with their feelings. It's totally normal for a two-year-old to throw a tantrum. However, suppose your child is older than five and is still exhibiting erratic behavior and constant meltdowns. In that case, it's a sign that they need help to manage their emotions. Teaching your child to identify their emotions will provide them with a fundamental framework, which helps them understand how they can deal with difficult emotions while staying within the limits of socially acceptable behavior.

You should also note that some children struggle to regulate their emotions more than others. For instance, children with ADHD, anxiety, or other issues may be prone to emotional outbursts and have difficulty managing their feelings. However, this does not in any way mean that they're incapable of learning to self-regulate. It just means that you have to try a little bit harder with them. When your kids act out, encourage them to slow down and reflect on their behavior instead of punishing them. This is what emotional regulation is all about. And this is where play therapy comes in.

How Play Therapy Can Help

Most children are known to have bad communication skills, which makes sense since they are young. Play therapy engages children in a way that makes them comfortable enough to open up about their feelings. It uses different tools, games, and toys to help them communicate their experiences and emotions nonverbally. Young children are naturally creative; play therapy considers this and provides them with the tools and space to express themselves creatively and honestly. Below are some play therapy techniques you can try with your children to help them express and regulate their feelings better.

1. Emotion Guessing Jar (Ages 4 and up)

This fun, engaging play therapy activity is designed to help children explore and understand their emotions. It will help them identify their emotions and what they look like.

Materials Needed:

- A clear jar or container with a lid
- Colored construction paper or cardstock
- Scissors
- Markers, crayons, or colored pencils
- Emotion word cards (e.g., happy, sad, angry, surprised, scared)
- Optional: Decorative stickers, glitter, or ribbons to embellish the jar

Instructions:

1. First, prepare the emotion guessing jar by decorating it with ribbons, glitter, paint, or stickers. You can ask your child to help you with this craft.
2. Next, cut the card into small rectangular pieces that can fit easily into the jar. Each piece should be large enough to write a single emotion word.
3. Using markers or crayons, write each emotion on a piece of paper while using a different color for each emotion. For instance, anger could be red, happiness could be blue, etc. Ensure you write plenty of emotions the children can identify and relate to.
4. Add a facial expression on each emotion card. You can draw these, use stickers, or print out the provided emotional expressions sheet. Fold the cards, or simply place them in the jar and mix them up.
5. Gather the participants for this game. This activity is best when multiple people participate, so try to get the whole family involved or ask your children's friends to participate.
6. Ask the youngest participant to pick a card from the jar without showing it to the others.
7. The participant should then be asked to act out or express the emotion written on the card without speaking. They should be encouraged to use body language, facial expressions, and gestures.
8. The other participants can take turns guessing what emotion is being portrayed.
9. As the activity progresses, ask each player to share a personal story or incident where they felt these emotions.

2. Expressing Grief through Storytelling (Ages 6 and up)

Storytelling can be a very effective way of getting children to express their emotions creatively. Whether it's you or your child telling the story, this activity always has a positive learning effect on the child. You can do this in a group or just with your child. This particular storytelling technique is to be used for children dealing with grief or loss.

Materials Needed:

- A children's storybook
- A piece of paper
- Drawing supplies
- Markers or pens for writing

Instructions:

1. Begin narrating the story to your child. You can use whatever story you find in a book or online or stick with the story provided for this activity.
2. Set the stage for the story and provide the beginning and middle of the storyline.
3. Then, ask your child to complete the story on their own. Depending on their age, they can either do this verbally or write it down.
4. Ask your child to draw a picture for the story as well.

Story:

"In a bustling city filled with skyscrapers and endless noise, there lived a young girl named Maya. Maya had a heart full of dreams and a mind that brimmed with curiosity. She was always eager to explore the wonders of the world. But one day, a heavy sadness descended upon Maya's world. Her beloved father, who had shared countless stories and laughter, passed away unexpectedly. The city seemed quieter, and Maya's spirit dimmed as she grappled with the weight of her grief.

In her sorrow, Maya discovered a dusty old cellphone that belonged to her grandfather. She switched it on, and to her surprise, she found a series of unread messages. Each message was filled with love, wisdom, and memories that her grandfather had carefully crafted before his passing. Driven by a desire to uncover the untold stories, Maya embarked on a journey through the city, following the clues left within the messages. She visited places her grandfather had mentioned - a hidden bookstore, a park bench by the river, and a cozy café that served his favorite hot chocolate.

As Maya explored, she encountered strangers who had crossed paths with her grandfather. They shared heartwarming stories about how he had touched their lives, leaving an indelible mark of kindness and compassion. One by one, Maya collected these stories, cherishing each connection to her grandfather. And with each tale, her sadness transformed into gratitude for the love he had shared and the impact he had made.

But here is where the story becomes a mystery, waiting for you to unlock its secret. What final message did Maya discover? How did it bring comfort and closure to Maya's grieving heart? It's up to you to complete the story. Use your imagination to unravel the mystery and bring a sense of peace to Maya's journey. Draw a picture or write a short paragraph expressing your ideas and feelings."

3. Emotion Thermometer (Ages 4 and up)

An emotion thermometer will help your child identify the intensity of their emotions. This is a visual tool that will help your child to rate their feelings. This activity encourages self-reflection and provides a platform for open discussions about emotions.

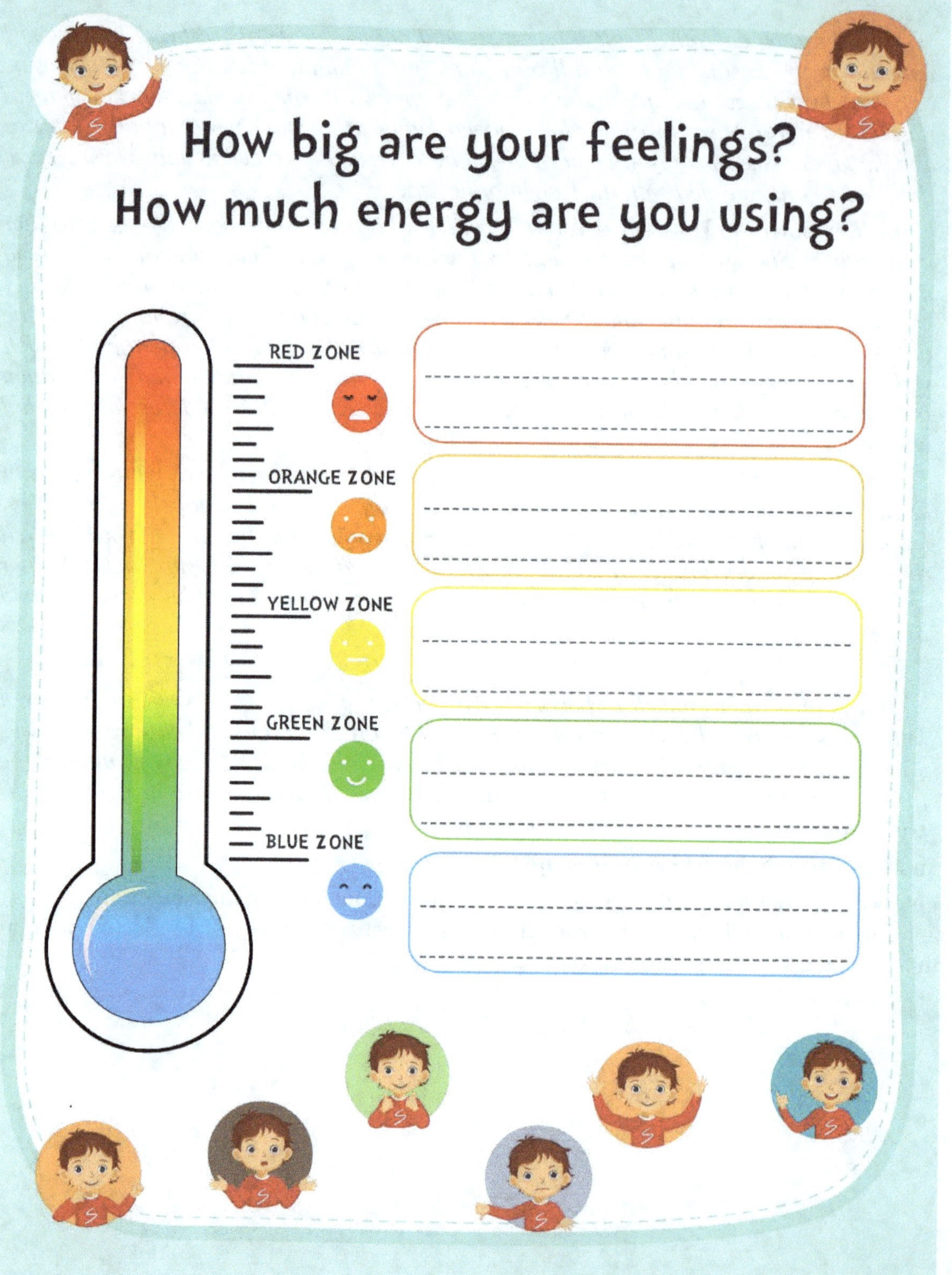
How big are your feelings?
How much energy are you using?
RED ZONE
ORANGE ZONE
YELLOW ZONE
GREEN ZONE
BLUE ZONE

Materials:

- Printable Emotion thermometer activity template (provided)

Instructions:

1. Since children are familiar with the idea of a thermometer, you will simply have to explain to them how an emotional thermometer works.
2. A feelings thermometer is just like any other thermometer, only it measures feelings instead of temperature.
3. At the top, you'll notice a frowning face with the number 10. If you rate something with this, it will mean that you feel very bad or anxious.
4. At the bottom, there's a smiling face, which means you don't feel anxious but feel good about a situation.
5. In the middle is a neutral face with no smile or frown. This is the medium face or when a child doesn't feel much.
6. The thermometer is divided into sections, and you can introduce more complex emotions as your child ages.
7. For example, when your child is young, they'll only know feelings like anger or sadness, but when they get older, they'll have feelings like frustration, resentment, etc.

4. Emotion Journaling (Ages 14 and up)

This activity is suitable for older children who have trouble regulating their emotions. It promotes self-reflection, emotional awareness, and personal growth. By practicing journaling, teens can explore and process their emotions in a safe and private space.

Materials Needed:

- Journal or notebook
- Pen or pencil
- Optional: Colored pencils, markers, or other art supplies for creative expression

Instructions:

1. Encourage your child to set aside some dedicated time to journal every day. This activity is most effective if done with consistency.
2. Gift your kid a writing journal or notebook and ask them to create an emotions diary or journal. Make it clear to them that you respect their privacy and will never try to breach it.
3. Talk to them about the benefits of emotional journaling and explain why it's so important to unload your feelings in a safe space.
4. Introduce some journal prompts to help them out. A few examples include:
   - Write about a time when you felt proud of yourself. What was your achievement, and how did it make you feel?
   - Reflect on a recent challenge or setback you experienced. How did it impact your emotional state, and what lesson did you learn from the situation?

- Describe someone who has greatly influenced you or who you admire. How would you describe your emotions when you think of them, and what is the reason behind those sentiments?
- Explore a recent situation that made you feel anxious or stressed. What triggered those emotions, and how did you cope with them?
- Consider a goal you have for yourself. Describe how achieving this goal will make you feel and what steps you can take to work towards it.

5. Encourage honest expression from your child. Explain to them that there are no right or wrong answers when journaling. This practice is for no one but them. So, there's no need to suppress emotions or hide their real thoughts.

5. Emotional Bingo (Ages 8 and up)

Emotional bingo is a fun and interactive game for children to develop emotional awareness and learn to identify their emotions. There are about 25 emotions mentioned in this bingo chart, which will also help improve your child's emotional vocabulary.

BINGO

		★		

EMOTIONS CARDS

EMOTIONS CARDS

Materials Needed:

- Bingo game (provided)
- Emotion cards (provided)
- Velcro attachments
- Bingo chips

Instructions:

1. The emotion cards have every emotion mentioned and illustrated on them, as well as a number in the top right-hand corner. Print out these cards and paste them onto cardboard cutouts for durability.
2. Finally, print out the bingo board sheets according to the number of players in the game.
3. Attach the calling cards onto the feelings chart in their respective places using Velcro.
4. Finally, hand out the bingo cards and chips to the players. Give each player a bingo board and begin the game.
5. Start the game by having each player place a chip on the center square, which is empty.
6. Call out a number and the emotion that goes with it. If a player has the card for this emotion, they will raise their hand.
7. Ask them to tell the group about a time they felt this emotion, and then place a bingo chip on that number on their bingo board.
8. The first one to get a line filled across, down, or diagonally wins.

Through play therapy, children are given the opportunity to explore and understand their emotions in a playful and non-threatening manner. By teaching children practical coping skills and providing them with a repertoire of self-regulation techniques, you empower them to navigate the complexities of their emotions. By incorporating playfulness, creativity, and empathy, you can guide your children toward healthier emotional development, increased self-awareness, and a brighter path to emotional well-being.

Chapter 6: Child-Centered Group Play Therapy

Child-centered Group Play Therapy (CCGPT) is a specialized and valuable type of therapy that uses group play to help children explore and learn about their emotions as well as how to socialize. Trained therapists lead children in playing together in a risk-free and inviting setting.

Let's discuss what this kind of therapy involves and how it can help children manage their emotions and maintain friendships. Many concepts make this treatment effective, but it's always vital to have a safe and inviting environment for this therapy. There are different activities based on CCGPT, like using theme-based play arts and telling stories with each other as a group.

CCGPT is a very helpful and fun experience for children.

https://www.pexels.com/photo/preschool-children-doing-hand-exercise-with-teachers-8613366/

Child-Centered Group Play Therapy

The Child-Centered Group Play Therapy (CCGPT) program is a therapeutic treatment aimed at helping young children aged between 3 and 10 with problems with social-emotional behaviors and relational concerns. It uses the language of play, which is natural for children and therapeutic relationships, to develop a risk-free and consistent setting where they can thrive.

This setting permits youngsters to feel completely accepted and understood while they process their internal experiences and feelings via the use of play and games. Furthermore, CCGPT encourages youngsters to practice brand-new social and coping skills while engaging with two to three team members.

Benefits of Child-Centered Group Play Therapy

Child-Centered Group Play Treatment (CCGPT) provides an innovative outlet for children to show their feelings without fear or disappointment. If you want to use CCGPT for your child, consider some of its advantages listed below.

- **It Is a Safe Space**

By taking part in this treatment, children have a safe and non-threatening space to reveal their sensations to a certified expert. This group therapy is a smooth bridge between imagination and reality while helping young children display their emotions. Subsequently, the specialist can evaluate their non-verbal cues to help figure out and reduce any kind of unhealthy psychological habits exhibited by the children. This treatment is particularly useful when children struggle to express their anxieties to their guardians or loved ones.

- **The Therapy Boosts Self-Esteem**

This therapy also supports children facing challenging life experiences such as natural catastrophes, domestic violence, or even injury. Play therapy allows children to learn healthy and balanced approaches to managing their feelings and handling various difficult scenarios. Work-related specialists and social workers normally take advantage of this type of play therapy, which can contribute to the children's positive mental wellness and overall well-being in their care.

- **It Builds Problem-Solving Abilities**

Children may develop independent analytic skills. They create their scenarios with playthings and games and frequently work toward dealing with small or substantial problems through role-playing. Therapists also present youngsters with issues they can address individually in this type of play therapy. For example, they may provide a child with a situation or ask, "What would you do if Teddy ate hedgehog's food without approval?" The child's reaction to such a scenario may offer some understanding of their skills and behaviors learned from home.

- **Kids can Make Use of Play Therapy to Learn Life Skills**

When youngsters participate in group play therapy, they learn to handle difficult feelings and navigate various situations. In addition, they learn how to develop positive behaviors and communicate with others in a healthy, balanced, and respectful way. By dealing with accredited psychological health experts, they gain a new understanding of their thoughts and emotions. CCGPT is an efficient and safe means for kids to handle family concerns, medical situations, and other stressful life experiences. For children battling early-life adversity, group play therapy is a safe method for them to discover their feelings and coping mechanisms without feeling bewildered.

- **Group Therapy Teaches Responsibilities**

Playing is a helpful way for children to create a sense of responsibility. By participating in different group play therapies, children discover how to take responsibility for their actions and decisions while also discovering that they are not responsible for everything that happens. Furthermore, cleaning up after play sessions shows healthy organizational abilities and responsibility.

- **It Helps with Making Friends**

Connecting with peers can be testing for people of different ages, but CCGPT helps children learn and develop social abilities. During these play therapy sessions, the specialist will guide them through different tasks to promote favorable social interactions and lower hostility. As a result of developing these skills, children may also discover that making and maintaining friendships is less complicated. For any child experiencing social anxiety or shyness, play therapists give support that facilitates socializing with other children going through different group play activities.

Activities That Can Be Incorporated into CCGPT

The following are some activities you can incorporate into Child-Centered Group Play Therapy:

- **Group Storytelling**

In play therapy groups for children, group storytelling is an animated activity that stimulates creativity through collaborations within the community. This activity helps promote a sense of belonging. Each child engaged in this activity has an opportunity to enhance communication skills while developing problem-solving strategies alongside new social interactions with peers.

Children participate while taking turns contributing individual sentences that help shape the overall storyline, thus building great listening and narrative skills. The nature of this activity supports extensive imaginative exploration, as every contribution makes way for new possibilities added by any participant, fostering empathy for the needs of other kids while also learning to respect different perspectives.

In CCGPT, group storytelling provides a multitude of benefits for children. First and foremost, it enhances their communication skills by promoting verbal expression, active listening, and turn-taking. Through working together to create stories, children also learn to collaborate, cooperate, and respect each other's contributions. It also encourages empathy and understanding as children engage with diverse perspectives and experiences.

The process of crafting a story as a team stimulates creativity and teamwork while nurturing imaginative thinking in children. Also, engaging in group storytelling sessions presents opportunities for children to navigate challenges and solve problems within the narrative context while developing social interaction skills like sharing and supporting others.

- **Color Therapy**

Having fun with colors is a remarkable way to help children loosen up and also have fun. This therapy is terrific since it involves vivid tools, which every child enjoys. You will need Skittles or M&M's for this task, and you will share them with the kids and their loved ones. After that, tell them to arrange the candies by shade and based on the variety of colors. Then, ask them to address some prompts like the following:

- The green candies describe their family in words
- The orange candies explain what needs improvement in their family
- For the red candies, ask them to express their worries
- Use yellow candies to prompt them to speak about their favorite memories
- When it comes to purple candies, ask them to define fun activities that their family takes pleasure in

- **Clay Therapy**

Having fun with clay can be a valuable way for children to reveal themselves artistically and show their feelings. By modeling the clay, they release stress and anxiety while also creating objects that represent their psychological health and wellness struggles. For therapists, observing the results of this activity can give important insights that can lead to prospective solutions.

- **Painting Therapy**

Similarly, painting can also be a restorative tool for children to use. The liberty to produce whatever they want with their fingers provides a sense of control and an outlet for their feelings. As therapists observe the child's painting, they try to understand what it stands for in relation to the child's life and psychological state.

- **Family Drawing Therapy**

Illustrating their family is another useful task in play therapy, and through this, the child is urged to explain what each family member stands for and what they think of them. The therapist can get a clearer understanding of the role of each member of the family and see how they affect the child by asking some relevant questions based on their drawing. The child's unique perspective in their drawing can reveal hidden emotions that they may not have been otherwise able to verbalize.

- **Theme-Based Play**

Group plays (based on a certain theme) involve making a space that offers relevance to a certain subject, permitting the young ones to try and join in events connected to that theme. In group play therapy aimed at children, theme-based play is valuable for teaching self-expression, psychological control, and analytic ability. The therapist can establish a varied and exciting play space by selecting styles that resonate with the child's experiences or passions, allowing them to explore and grow.

The themes can be broad, varying from community-oriented play to animal-related tasks. Each task offers unique opportunities for the children to enjoy imaginative play, act out different duties, narrate, and express themselves creatively. Specialists can enhance the children's participation and create a more immersive therapeutic environment by integrating materials and props that connect to the chosen style.

Engaging with pets can also be a fun play task for children in play therapy. A pet care center can be developed using pets and pet treatment supplies where kids can take turns pretending to be veterinarians or pet dog owners. Animal-themed puppets are effective tools to promote communication and self-expression during this play treatment. By making pet shows, youngsters can develop imaginative stories and also develop their imagination and storytelling abilities.

Developing animal habitats by using art supplies and figurines teaches kids about pet habitats, biodiversity, and ecological control. Furthermore, animal-themed yoga poses and activities can promote psychological proficiency, compassion, understanding, self-regulation, and relaxation. Finally, visiting a local zoo or animal haven offers an experiential learning opportunity for children to observe and connect with a variety of pets, fostering interest, empathy, and connection with the natural environment.

- **Communication Game**

This is a popular game for kids' therapy, and it is similar to board games. You start by placing little pieces on the board, and after taking turns rolling a die and moving the pieces, you select a card that tells you what to talk about concerning how you're really feeling or what to do next. The rule is to comply with the guidelines on the card and gain the most chips by the end of the game. This is a great method to find out what's going on with the child inside and help them speak about their feelings securely and happily.

Other CCGPT Techniques

This section will show you other simple and effective child-centered group play therapy techniques that can be easily incorporated into your sessions with kids.

Laughter

Laughter seems so simple, yet it can be a wonderful exercise for the heart, so why not integrate it into play therapy? You can incorporate this technique by playing a tickling game or sharing funny stories and jokes that could encourage the children to laugh. This can help gain an understanding of their family dynamic if you're conscious enough to observe their reaction to what is said and how it is said. True feelings can be expressed in a happy and free environment; laughter is all you need to bring out these feelings.

Toys

Stressful situations can also be played out by using toys to help children feel a lot more comfortable. As a therapist, you already know how vital it is to assist youngsters through these difficult situations and improve their self-confidence and sense of control. So toys are what you need to help these kids through these stressful situations.

Games

Integrating easy games like hide-and-seek during play therapy sessions can provide insight into a child's mood, revealing concealed feelings of stress and anxiety. Magic tricks can act as an excellent ice breaker, helping children to feel more comfortable and in control during their therapy sessions. By teaching them tricks and allowing them to execute those tricks, children can improve their self-confidence and also use their creativity. It is absolutely vital to keep play therapy sessions fun and allow kids to open up and feel in control.

To sum up, CCGPT is a valuable therapy for understanding kids and helping them manage their emotions. In this approach, children can discover their feelings and develop essential life skills through a series of tasks and also play in a secure and welcoming setting. This play therapy method is about putting the child first and treating them with concern and respect, which helps with emotional expression, analytic abilities, social development, self-confidence, and compassion. The treatment sessions include activities like theme-based play, art therapy, and group narration that make it satisfying for kids to participate. Ultimately, CCGPT helps children to get the help they need to grow and succeed.

Chapter 7: Play Therapy in Neurodiversity

This chapter focuses on how play therapy can be adapted to meet the needs of children with neurodiverse conditions like autism spectrum disorder, ADHD, and sensory processing disorder. By understanding the special needs of these children and adapting play therapy techniques and activities, it is possible to create a safe and effective therapeutic environment that supports their development and emotional well-being.

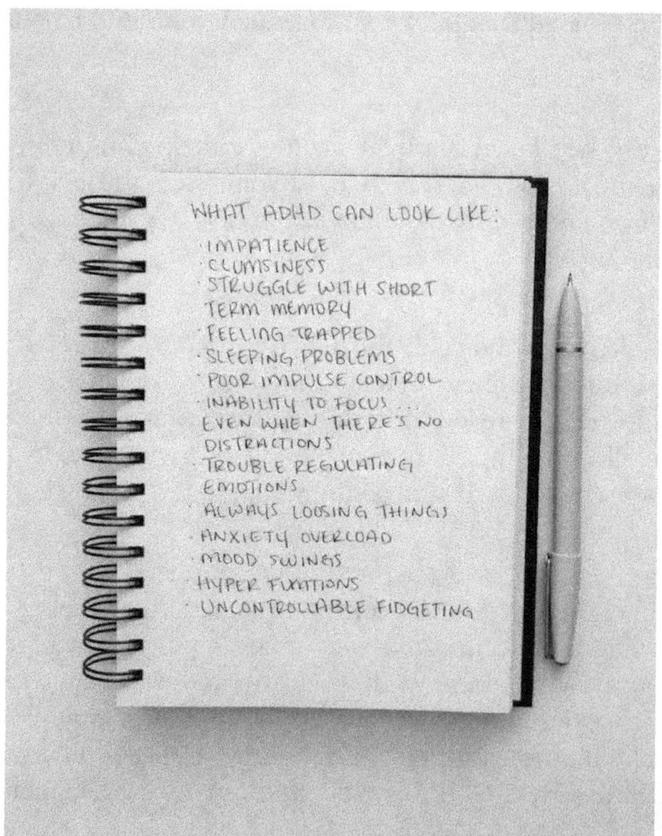

Children with ADHD can greatly benefit from play therapy.

https://www.pexels.com/photo/a-notebook-with-notes-about-adhd-8378749/

What Are Neurodiverse Conditions?

To understand the role of play therapy in neurodiversity treatment, it's a good idea to explore the different neurodiverse conditions. Understanding how these conditions impact a child's development, behavior, and communication skills will direct the therapist to specific play therapy activities that are effective for children with neurodiverse conditions.

Neurodiverse is an umbrella term used for people with differences in brain development. These differences affect how their brain chemistry works. Neurodiverse people have numerous strengths but also have their kryptonite. Also, their challenges often differ from neurotypicals (those without atypical brain development). For example, they often have better memory, visualization, and problem-solving skills. However, they often struggle with learning disabilities, socio-emotional development, and mental health conditions. They can also have short-term, recurrent, and chronic conditions and physical disabilities.

Because neurodiversity impacts people differently, people with the same condition can have very different symptoms, not to mention that several conditions have degrees, depending on the severity of their symptoms and the amount of assistance they require.

Some of the conditions most common among the neurodiverse include:

- **Autism spectrum disorder** (including **Asperger's syndrome)** -comes with a broad range of symptoms, from communication and attention issues to emotional dysregulation and other problems.
- **Attention-deficit hyperactivity disorder (ADHD)** - These individuals have trouble focusing on tasks for a sufficient amount of time, which disrupts their everyday lives.
- **Down's syndrome** - A genetic condition that causes a plethora of cognitive, behavioral, and physical symptoms and developmental delay.
- **Dyscalculia** (difficulty with math), **dysgraphia** (difficulty with writing), **dyslexia** (difficulty with reading), and **dyspraxia** (difficulty with coordination).
- Mental health conditions like **obsessive-compulsive disorder, bipolar disorder,** and others.
- **Prader-Willi syndrome** - A genetic condition that causes disproportional development of body parts, developmental and behavioral symptoms, and sleep issues.
- **Sensory processing disorders** - The individual has trouble processing the sensory stimuli they receive from the environment, which drives their brain to overload, causing overstimulation or under-stimulation.
- **Social anxiety**. A specific type of anxiety disorder is a mental health condition that manifests in subjective symptoms like feelings of nervousness, panic, and fear and physical signs like sweating and a rapid heartbeat.
- **Tourette syndrome** - A neurodevelopmental disorder that causes the individual to make involuntary sounds and movements known as ticks. These often stunt socio-emotional development.
- **Williams syndrome** - A unique genetic condition that manifests in severe cognitive delays, physical symptoms like heart conditions, and unusual physical features.

Sensory Play Activities

Many of the conditions mentioned above come with sensory issues. Sensory play activities can be helpful for children who have sensory processing disorders. Here are some benefits of these activities:

- Promote language skills development by getting the child to talk, role play, and express their emotions
- Improves brain function by creating more neural pathways through adequate sensory stimulation
- Hones social skills through sharing, listening, and taking play
- Teaches self-regulation - how to respond to sensory stimulation in a more adequate way
- Due to the physical elements, the activities can improve fine and gross motor skills and coordination, strengthening muscles and hand-eye coordination.

Below are a few recommended activities for sensory play therapy.

Finger, Footprint, and Food Painting

Painting their fingers or feet and leaving their prints on a surface is a wonderful way for children to express themselves. Give them a piece of paper and watercolors, set it on top of a newspaper, and let the child's imagination go free while creating art with their hands and feet.

Food painting is a less messy and great activity for children who like to put everything in their mouths. Give the child soft foods like yogurt, chocolate sauce, apple puree, blackberries, and other foods he/she likes to taste/smell/touch (varied textures) and let them create their art safely. It's a good idea to provide pinafores.

Playing with Slime or Playdough

Make these yourself if you're worried about the child swallowing slime or play-dough. Mix water and cornflower for the slime, and add edible glitter and coloring. Make sure you create a mixture that shifts from liquid to solid as the child plays with it. You can make play-dough from pasta and add a natural scent and a flavor like peppermint, lemon, cinnamon, vanilla, or any other fragrance the child prefers.

Can you make your own musical instrument? You might want to make a shaker, a drum, a guitar or something else of your own choice.

Here are some resources you may want to use. Remember you can think of your own ideas too.

Kitchen roll
Scissors
Glue
Tape
Tissue paper
Plastic or paper cups
Boxes of different size
Lentils or other dried beans
Elastic bands of different thicknesses

Draw a picture of your creation.

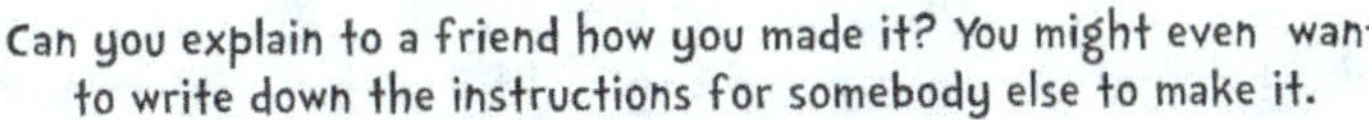

Pour rice inside a strong balloon or plastic bottle, or use wooden spoons and a bucket for a DIY drum set, and you'll have instruments that enhance sensory stimulation. Alternatively, you can fill a box with sand, water, toy fish, shells, and other water-themed items to create a sensory ocean. This has been proven to have a calming effect on children's senses while they can still enjoy splashing water or swirling it with their hands.

Hide Toys in Jell-O (or dry beans, pasta, or rice)

If your child likes to play with goo/slime - or loves Jell-O - you can try hiding toys inside this wobbly substance. Simply make the liquid jelly/goo or Jell-O, place small toys into the jelly molds, cover them with your chosen substance, and let it solidify in the fridge. Encourage your child to dig in and get their toys out of the substance.

Make a Pouring Station

Pour water into different-sized containers, bottles, cups, and jugs, and place them into a larger container or bathtub. Alternatively, you can add different food coloring to the water to enhance the experience. The child should pour water from one place to another and mix the colors.

Social Skill Enhancing Games

Games focusing on social skills, such as taking turns, sharing, and communication, can be helpful for children with autism spectrum disorder or other neurodiverse conditions. Below are some of the most recommended games.

The Staring Contest

Children with ASD and other conditions affecting socio-emotional development often have difficulty maintaining eye contact because they find it uncomfortable and easily overwhelmed. The staring contest is an activity that allows children to get used to looking at the person they're talking to by encouraging this behavior in simple steps. Here is how to teach it to your child:

1. Look at your child and ask them to look into your eyes for 3-5 seconds.
2. If they manage this or can hold even longer eye contact, offer them praise for positive reinforcement.
3. However, if your child can't stare at you for the amount of time you've allocated, don't force them, as this will only cause them to become more anxious. This is not good because being forced to stare at you in the first place is probably taxing enough for them.
4. Instead, get a pair of stickers that look like eyes and stick them on your forehead. Then, encourage your child to look at your forehead instead of your eyes. It will be less awkward for them - and they will still look at your face, which is an improvement.
5. Whether the child was looking into your eyes during your exercises or into the sticker eyes, complement them at the end of the exercise to reinforce positivity.

Trying Out the Face Game

This is another fantastic way to encourage improvement in your child's social skills. And it's very easy. You just need to make faces and encourage your child to mimic your facial expressions.

Instructions:

1. Start with an action the child can copy easily. For example, you can cup your face while rolling your eyes. Or touch your nose while drawing your cheeks in.

2. Make a few funny facial expressions once your child learns to mimic what you're doing. If your child struggles to identify other people's feelings, mimicking facial expressions will help them learn how emotions are expressed.
3. Alternate between different expressions, showing how they look on a person's face so that the child knows what to look for when reading other people.
4. Name the emotions tied to the expressions and ask your child to imitate you.

The Name Game

Besides helping your child learn to introduce themselves, this activity will allow them to learn the names of others around them. You can play this game with your child and involve friends and family members.

Instructions:

1. Gather everyone in a circle so all of you can see each other.
2. Look at the child and say your name out loud while pointing a finger at yourself.
3. Then, encourage the person to your right to mimic your action, and the person to their right to do the same, and so on, until everyone in the circle has introduced themselves.

Game Etiquette

Neuro-diverse children often have issues following the game etiquette, like waiting for their turn, getting upset when they lose, etc. This simple activity is designed to teach children the importance of being polite when playing a game with others.

Instructions:

1. Pick any game that you or your child can play, for example, a board game.
2. Before you start playing the game, ask the child to shake hands with you, look into your eyes (or face if they're uncomfortable with eye contact), and say: "Good luck!"
3. Once the game ends, your child should repeat the actions above, except they should substitute "Good luck!" with "Good game!"
4. If your child refuses to do this before or after the game, tell them this means that the game will be void.
5. Your child will probably get upset at the first few attempts, but they will soon learn that they must repeat those steps if they want to keep their score (and have a good experience).

Learning Emotions

Print and play cards depicting emotions to help the child learn to recognize and read other people's feelings properly.

Instructions:

1. Name each emotion on the cards and let the child observe them. Repeat the naming if necessary.
2. Then, ask them to name the emotions themselves.
3. They may get confused or unsure about reading some of the feelings because they don't know what they're called or can't remember. If this happens, offer a context for the emotion they've failed to name. Alternatively, you can describe the feeling to them. For instance, you can explain that the card showcasing the "excited" emotion signifies the happiness someone feels when anticipating something good.

Animal-Assisted Therapy

Animal-assisted play therapy is beneficial for children with a range of neurodiverse conditions. During this type of therapy, children interact with animals, which positively affects their social, cognitive, and emotional well-being.

Animal-assisted therapy has been found to help as follows:

- It can reduce anxiety-induced physical symptoms like pain, elevated heart rate, and blood pressure.
- It can help children to deal with feelings related to distress and depression.
- It can enhance social and communication skills.

When interacting with animals, the children know they are in a caring environment. They can talk to the animals, play with them, and touch them without feeling judged. They feel warm, comforted, and tend to laugh a lot, reducing their anxiety. After animal-assisted therapy, children are often more playful, focused, and social than before. They can be motivated to interact socially with people and hone their communication skills.

Card Games for Socio-Emotional Development

"Step into Conversation" is a simple - yet incredibly helpful - card game made for children with autism, helping them learn how to talk to others appropriately and carry on a conversation with perspective and empathy.

The game comes with sets of footprints, cards with simple instructions, and a set of numbers of additional topics the child can add to the conversations. Here is how the game works:

1. The child should step on the footprint you placed on the floor - opposite the footprint you or another person will be occupying. This ensures they stay in one place and will stop turning and moving around.
2. Give the child a card and get them to read the instructions on one side. These include commands like stand, look, talk, and listen. Remind the child that they need to follow the instructions.
3. Ask the child to keep reading the card. They will find sentences they need to finish. For example:

"Hi.... (The person's name they're talking to)."

"I would like to ... (what they want to do)."

"Would you like to ... with me?" (Do or replace with the action they referenced previously).

1. After each sentence, the child should stop and listen to the other person's answer (there is a visual reminder of this on the card).
2. If the child has trouble taking their turn asking their question, remind them to look at the first commands on the card.
3. Once they master the three-sentence activity, you can ask the child how many things they want to add to the conversation. Ask them to select a number from the sticker's sheet and place it onto their card. They will only be allowed to say as many additional sentences or ask as many additional questions as the number on their cards indicates.

Step into Conversation helps improve the following skills:

- Improving social relationships
- Making eye contact
- Initiating conversation and staying on topic during conversations
- Asking relevant questions and answering them appropriately
- Taking turns talking and listening

Movement Activities

Movement activities, like yoga or dance, can be ideal for children with ADHD or other conditions that involve hyperactivity or impulsivity.

Benefits of gross motor skills include:

- **Improved chemical activity in the brain** - Movement promotes the release of endorphins, the happiness hormones that also make the brain more pliable and more receptive to new information.
- **Improved coordination skills** - Physical activities require the person to use both sides of their brain, which improves balance, accuracy, and coordination.
- **Improved physical health** - Exercising motor skills helps to build muscle tone and allows for better bone density and regular heart rate, blood pressure, and breathing rate.
- **Improved social skills** - Physical activities often involve engaging with others; this helps teach children how to socialize easily.

Below are a few ideas for movement activities for neuro-diverse children.

Playing Ball

Many children like to play with balls, so you can use this simple exercise in many ways. For example:

- You can get a bouncing ball and play with your child by rolling, bouncing, tossing, or catching the ball between the two of you.
- Get a handball or tennis ball and toss it back and forth with your child.
- Get a small sheet and place a beach ball or other ball onto it. Make the ball bounce around by having you and the child move the sheet up and down.

Replace Tables with Walls

If your child spends much time sitting at the table being creative, get something like a magnetic board, materials you can stick to a board, and similar items you can put on the walls. Your child can still be creative, but they will now have to engage their entire body because they will be standing up and moving in front of the wall.

Dancing

Music is great for improving motor skills. Play your child's favorite music or videos, and encourage them to sing and dance. For smaller children, there are great songs that help them learn body parts while listening to music. You can add your own spin to it by asking your child to step, balance, or jump at different times.

Yoga

Yoga is a mindfulness exercise that helps build awareness, strength, balance, and flexibility. Provided it's engaging enough, it also boosts focus and attention. Look for a program suitable for your child's abilities and age range.

Chapter 8: Play Therapy for Adolescents

Children are often creative when allowed to play on their own. They act out the emotions and feelings of imaginary characters and also express feelings they've been exposed to in one way or another. This makes the play therapy method much more effective with them than with adults. Surprisingly, this also works on adolescents. Growing into a young adult will naturally mean their method of play changes with time. It tends to be more organized than fantasized. As a parent or caregiver, you must be flexible enough to use different methods depending on your child's age and interests.

Your children's methods of play will evolve as they grow up.

https://www.pexels.com/photo/a-young-boy-sitting-on-his-bed-while-playing-ukulele-7573225/

As they become adolescents, children's minds start to wander off on abstract thoughts as they become more involved in new and creative things. Young adolescents sometimes even enjoy custom playing, and some find board games more entertaining. As a parent, you should be aware of this minor interest so that you can guide them properly.

In this chapter, you'll discover the many ways play therapy can serve as an effective tool for helping adolescents develop emotional regulation, social skills, and a positive sense of self. You will also learn about their many opportunities at this age and how therapy plays a role in their emotional, social, and cognitive changes.

An Adolescent Stage of Development

The stage of adolescence is when a child transcends into near adulthood. The world is now viewed in a different light, and during this stage, their body changes first, then the thoughts and hormonal changes kick in, and this often happens too fast. These changes greatly affect their social, sexual, and cognitive behaviors. So, as a guardian, you should be aware of what to expect at each stage of development and have a plan of how to provide a healthy lifestyle for each developmental stage.

As a child grows into adulthood, they tend to want to decide what values to uphold, and they now feel the need for more independence. They are hopeful about what lies ahead and base most of their decisions on emotions, not realities. As they grow, so does their distance emotionally and physically from families and even their parents. But this isn't always so, as some, after this adjustment, still acknowledge the need for a greater bond with their parents. Perhaps they now realize the need for certain advice they still need for the future and hope for a more mature discussion with you rather than just an authoritarian one.

Here are the stages of adolescence and what changes to expect for each stage:

- **Early Adolescence (Ages 10 to 13)**

From this age, children start to grow really fast. They begin to notice physical body changes such as pubic hair under the armpits and around their genitals, deeper voice, breast growth in females, and testicle enlargement in males. The females have much earlier changes in many cases. Puberty may even begin as early as eight years old, and they may experience an early menstrual cycle. Due to these body changes, they may get more curious about certain things if they're not sure what to expect or what is considered "normal."

These children's thoughts are on a singular course. It's either left or right, black or white. There is little to no ground for indecision. To them, you're either good or bad, right or wrong. It's normal that they think only of themselves at this age. At this stage, they also succumb to peer pressure because they feel too conscious of their appearance and how they're viewed. They also begin to live more in isolation, and need privacy, and may even want to be free of their family.

- **Middle Adolescence (Ages 14 to 17)**

The bodily changes continue. By this age, physical changes may have been nearly complete for females. For males, there is more depth in voice and some acne development. Teens at this stage begin to grow interested in sexual relationships and companionship. There's the desire to explore identity and sexuality. With this curiosity, they will need your help, more than ever, to decide on relationship issues. You shouldn't make them feel uncomfortable. They could be led to other less savory activities if they don't get satisfactory answers. As they strive for more personal independence, they tend to disagree more with guardians and caregivers. They may spend most of their time with friends rather than family. Peer pressure is at its most forceful, and the struggle for social acceptance is real.

With all these changes going on, there is still a chasm between a mid-teen and an adult. Decisions can often have a lasting impact, and if they're not carefully channeled by someone your teen respects, they could have dire results. Best friends do not always have the life experience to be wise counselors, so parents must be aware of what is happening in their child's life. In the development of the brain, the frontal lobes grow last, which plays a big role in coordinating a person's decision-making, problem-solving abilities, and impulse control. And this growth will only be complete at the late stage of adolescence.

At this middle adolescence stage, they can think ahead but lack the will or impulse to actualize it. For example, they may think thoughts like:

"Why do I need to study? I could get answers while sitting close to XXX......'

"My girlfriend is on birth control pills; I do not need to use a condom."

"I could skip class and go hang out with friends; it's no big deal."

As a parent or caregiver, it's your responsibility to talk to them about the dangers of living recklessly and to explain why it's important to seek your advice whenever they want to make decisions.

- **Late Adolescents (18-21... and beyond!)**

At this stage, they have completed every major physical development and reached full adult height. Now, they can make more impulse-controlled decisions, take calculated risks, and understand the rewards for every action. With this in mind, they may have thoughts like:

"Why am I even watching this movie? I have exams and need to study."

"I should probably wear a condom to be 100% safe in preventing a pregnancy."

"If I get so high on this drug, it may take a toll on me the next day."

Help Your Adolescents Feel Comfortable Opening Up

Giving adolescents a platform for communication can prove to be a difficult process sometimes. They need to figure out their new emotions and understand the best ways to express them. When they're given a chance to express themselves without feeling unwelcome, they would be able to make sense of any future experience. Here are tips to help build a bridge of communication with teens:

- **Ask Them Questions:** It doesn't have to be direct and private, but letting them know you care about all that concerns them seems to stir up a hidden interest in them to open up. The only catch is that you need to be honest, patient, and compassionate in counsel.
- **Listen Without Judging Them:** When they finally open up to you, it's best you do most of the listening and not talking. Sometimes, they just need a listening ear to rant to, not that they necessarily need advice. Even adults can be that way sometimes. Unless they honestly request or desire it, just be the ear they cry to.
- **Encourage Healthy Communication Skills:** As a parent, you're the first model your kids look and learn from. You would need to develop good listening skills, respectful language, healthy ways of expressing thoughts and having constructive feelings before encouraging your kid to do likewise.
- **Create a Safe Space:** Adolescents need to feel comfortable and welcomed if they are to hold a conversation in the first place. When they sense the absence of such, they would gradually shy away.

Play Therapy Can Be an Effective Tool for Helping Adolescents

As a parent, you must have thought about whether or not therapy serves a great purpose in your teen's life. The notion that a therapy session plainly involves one person sitting, arms crossed, and making boring gestures just to get to the end of the meeting is entirely untrue. In fact, this isn't true at all for play therapy.

One other disturbing rumor is that play therapy is only dedicated to helping children aged 10 and below. You should know that teens and children share similar characteristics in this case. Both groups of children find it hard to express their feelings in words. Remember that teenagers will find their way around something once they sense it obstructs their freedom. But play is their freedom, so no worries here.

Here's one interesting fact about play. In whichever form it comes, either card games, board games, art, or numerous other therapeutic activities, it's proven effective in dealing with stress levels, building self-confidence, dealing with anxiety and depression, increasing problem-solving skills, coping skills, and much more. When all these are achieved, they can freely express their thoughts without feeling judged, whether they require healing from their past or from social or behavioral issues.

Another valid reason play therapy works amazingly well is that it eliminates any attempt for them to guess a response and crack their heads for answers that don't exist. Typical teen questions are why they feel what they feel and do what they do. Play therapy allows them to express feelings and emotions without breaking a sweat for words. The skills learned during such times can be applied in whatever settings they find themselves in.

Play Therapy Specializes in Using Play as a Medium for Healing and Communication

As mentioned before, play therapy serves to help build the emotional regulation of adolescents. Intense physical, emotional, mental, and social changes may cause challenges in expressing their feelings. Play therapy provides your adolescent a warm and safe environment with different tools for such expressions. It builds them up socially.

How is this possible?

Well, since teenagers often struggle with identity crises and often give in to peer pressure and conflict resolution and have a bit of a communication barrier, with play therapy, they can star in active play roles in or outside school and other interactive activities. This will give them a place to practice and develop their social skills. And with group talks, they can also watch others talk and take turns to share their experiences. All of this activity creates a safe space to learn, make mistakes, acquire new skills, and, of course, build healthy relationships.

Unique Challenges and Opportunities of Adolescence

With more room for friends comes more opportunities to decide when and with whom they will spend most of their time. This developmental challenge in teenagers has now been proven to be not only because of their biological changes but because other factors are involved. This age group has proven difficult, but looking closer, what stage of a person's life is without difficulties? Although these years are challenging, they should be considered normal, as with all age groups. Your adolescent will definitely grow out of them. It's a phase they must pass through to build them up for other stages of difficulties. They mustn't ignore these difficulties but simply embrace them as part of life. As a parent, guardian, or caregiver, you're meant to be there as such situations arise and come to their aid effectively when needed. Adolescents have cognitive behaviors, too, and it could be:

- How they view the world
- How they interact with those around them
- How they participate in groups or discussions

And all these differ from adulthood in that they greatly influence their decision-making skills.

How Does Play Therapy Key Affect These Factors?

Play therapy creates a supportive environment, and your adolescent can engage in interactive activities to help them come out of their shells. They also get to navigate their feelings and emotions through the diverse play techniques you set. Remember that there is no limitation as to which activities they can try. The following are some other challenges and how play therapy affects each stage.

Cognitive Challenges

During their development, they're unable to make fully conscious decisions alone. They struggle with abstract thoughts, problem-solving, and decision-making skills. This may be due to their sudden impulsivity and diverted thinking patterns. This can be dealt with using play therapy. With puzzles, games, acting, art storytelling, and much more, their cognitive abilities, which are responsible for their intelligence and problem-solving skills, are developed.

Identify Crises

Aside from the turmoil of emotions they feel at this stage, there is the challenge of self-discovery. No age group has more indecision than this one. Because of their struggle with identity, they look to society, family, and peers for affirmation. Play therapy introduces them to a safe environment for easy expression of ideas, thoughts, future aspirations, and identity exploration. With play therapy, they star in different roles during short plays to help them explore the many possibilities of characters and identify so they fit in the one perfect for them.

Discussed below are some potential play therapeutic activities designed for adolescents:

- **Art Therapy**

This provides a different means of communication. Art therapy may include drawing, craft making, painting, street painting (graffiti), college photo design, etc.

- **Group Therapy**

Group discussions help build social and interactive skills, empathy for others, and communication skills. Try these games during such sessions: short play (with individual roles) and team-building challenges.

- **Guarded Images and Board Games**

Try breathing exercises, short relaxation exercises, and even board games like chess, Scrabble, and Monopoly. These exercises build up their coping skills and emotional regulation and help reduce anxiety.

- **Try Tech**

Since most teenagers are tech-oriented, and this is a tech age, you can probably get them involved in play! Try playing video games, virtual reality experiences, or even use avatars for online role-playing games. This helps build their cognitive abilities and helps them to process emotions.

Play therapy is just as effective for any child, even in adolescence. As teenagers, there are a series of physical, mental, and emotional developments, creating a whole new experience for these young people. They become mentally and physically separated from family. They now care more about their appearance, so they move with peers with similar outlooks to fulfill their needs. Peer pressure affects teenagers more than any other factor that may confront them. Therefore, as parents, your teenagers should be introduced to a guided and safe method to help them build self-confidence and improve their emotional and social skills. Play therapy offers such an environment.

Every teenager has an expression barrier just like children do, and with an increasing need to be understood, they turn to addictions or things that are less suitable to help them. Introducing them to play therapy can be the best gift you could ever give them. Play therapy opens them to a world of creativity, fun, and a judgment-free environment. Unlike the standard therapy that only sets to question their past and feelings, here teenagers are given freedom and are exposed to activities such as games, custom playing roles, and so on to develop their strengths.

Chapter 9: Healing through Play: Addressing Trauma

Disclaimer: *This chapter is not intended to cure trauma or any mental disease. The parent/caregiver must seek a professional mental health advisor if their child is dealing with these problems.*

The science of play therapy is not as new as some think. This technique dates back about a hundred years and has become more recognized and prominent within the last 25 years.

Several studies and plenty of proof support the claims that it helps in the healing journeys of mental health patients, those afflicted by PTSD, domestic violence, anxiety, and troublesome behavior, to name a few. With very few exceptions, the techniques applied through play therapy have more often than not displayed positive results.

Play could be the form of healing your child is missing.

https://www.pexels.com/photo/woman-lying-on-the-floor-having-therapy-6998275/

Practitioners of play therapy usually focus on prevention and development. This means they focus on limiting the negative consequences that the child suffering from trauma might endure. They understand that they are most likely dealing with a person stuck in survival mode and that the reactions he/she is having are the expected reactions resulting from an unexpected event.

Children are not often as forthcoming and direct with their communication as adults. A therapist with a notepad and a lounge chair won't usually work to get the child to face their inner demons and negative experiences. That's where play therapy comes in. It gives the child the safe space and companionship to cultivate trust to be able to face their fears, overcome their shyness, and deal with the pain they endured.

Trauma

Many of the world's population have experienced unpleasant and upsetting events in their childhood. Though that is distressing, it doesn't necessarily mean they are all traumatized.

The agreed-upon definition is: an event or events that occur during your life that leaves you unable to cope, unable to move on, and leaves you feeling helpless.

Depending on their age, personality, and upbringing, each child reacts to trauma differently, even if they're siblings - and even if they're twins who suffered the same event. Odds are each has their own set of coping mechanisms that they tap into to be able to survive.

And each has to deal with the toll of set trauma on their body, mind, and relationships.

Be Bold
Be Brave
Be You

Trauma Triggers

Trauma can be caused by several factors, some of them are as follows;

- Natural disasters
- Bullying
- Sexual assault
- Domestic violence
- Conflict between caregivers
- War
- Witnessing violence or the passing of another
- Refugees
- Emotional manipulation and abuse

Trauma Symptoms

As mentioned before, young humans tend to have different coping methods to use when it comes to events that cause trauma. At times, symptoms of trauma are rather obvious and jarring. In other cases, they can be very subtle or barely noticeable. The descriptive symptoms are quite varied, such as the following:

- Repeated nightmares that may leave the child rather shaken
- Avoiding the memories of the event by occupying themselves with tasks to crowd their minds
- Avoiding individuals or locations that act as triggers of the trauma
- The child suffers from episodes in which they find themselves trapped in reliving the event.
- Severe anguish that may take too long to shake when the child is triggered by the memory (if they visit the place it occurred, for instance)
- Aggression
- Memory loss
- Issues in concentration
- Depression
- Sleeping disorders
- Being constantly on edge
- Becoming withdrawn
- Mood swings
- Attachment and detachment issues

The Role of the Caregiver

As parents responsible for a child who went through a traumatic event, it is very common to have a sense of helplessness, an urge to try anything to just "fix" your child. This can sometimes backfire in a way that may paint you as an inconsiderate adult – as if you are undermining their pain to make it seem smaller. Statements such as "It's not as bad as you think," or "You'll get over it," or "Try to be more positive" aren't as helpful as you may think.

There is a method called reflective listening, which is a bit more helpful and gives the child a sense of being heard and acknowledging their feelings. It's as easy as paraphrasing and restating the emotions and words that the other person is trying to communicate to you. "You're very distressed right now," "You're feeling helpless."

Always consider speaking with a professional. Having an expert help guide you in the healing process is always important. This is not the best time or situation to decide on spontaneity.

Being considerate, gentle, and kind when dealing with a distressed child is important. If they're being aggressive, isolating themselves, or showing behaviors inconsistent with their age or any other symptoms, know that these actions are their way of dealing and coping with their emotions and inner turmoil and accept the process.

The Role of Play Therapy

Using play and games allows the therapists to create an environment where there is no judgment, is safe, and allows a natural way to facilitate expression.

Children are taught ways to develop new and effective coping skills, and these enhance their resilience and are tools used to ease the recovery journey. They have their own space to deal with trauma without feeling pressured or overwhelmed.

Each child is provided with their own set of coping instruments, depending on personality and preference, like art or toys.

It allows them opportunities to regulate their emotions and tackle problems in a contained and healthy environment through using techniques like role play or storytelling.

It also allows them to step away from the trauma and deal with it in an indirect and figurative way, which is safer and more forgiving than other types of therapies.

Play therapy allows the child to move at their own speed, using methods with which they are comfortable, allowing them to explore their deeply buried emotions safely and face their own vulnerabilities while veering away from the possibility of traumatizing them again during the process of recovery.

Play Therapy Theories

Each therapist using play therapy usually follows one of these theories.

Child-Centered Play Therapy: Carl Rogers, the founder of this theory, believed that a huge significance and weight should be placed on the therapeutic relationship in order for the child to heal.

The therapist should make an effort to provide the child with a safe, empathetic environment to encourage the expression of emotions and allow them to feel accepted.

Jungian Play Therapy: This therapy relies on symbolism and its role in tapping into the subconscious mind of the child. Carl Jung, the creator of this method, believed that symbolism often used through sand play and art allows the child to express his/her feelings more openly and come to terms with the trauma they suffered.

Adlerian Play Therapy: This technique follows the belief that everyone has the capacity for improvement and change. It leans on the trusting relationship between the child and therapist and the process through which the therapist allows the child to face their actions and accept the consequences for them.

Filial Play Therapy: This method includes the caregiver/parent in the healing process of the child. The therapist coaches the parent on the different methods of play therapy suitable for their child to help enhance their relationship and improve their attachment.

It gives the child a sense of safety and support from their caregiver, promoting the healing journey.

Cognitive Behavioral Play Therapy: This Approach relies heavily on thoughts. The common understanding of the practice is that negative thoughts are likely to be primary triggers to the child's behavior. The therapist focuses on training the child to understand this concept and challenge these thoughts, empowering the child through problem-solving techniques and coping mechanisms.

Gestalt Play Therapy: This method allows the child to be rooted and aware of their emotions, thoughts, and physical sensations. It focuses on the now, using play and games to help the child unite his traumatic experience with his inner being.

COOTIE CATCHER
magic
unicorn
hearts
rainbow
1
2
3
4
5
6
7
8
You are some kind of wonderful.
Tell someone you love them.
What is a unicorns favorite type of story?
A fairy tale
Draw a picture of a rainbow and leave it for someone to find to make them smile.
You make my life magical.
What would you do if you encountered a unicorn?
What is you unicorn name?
Buttercup
Cloudberry
Dandelion
Bubbles
Like a unicorn: If you're lucky enough to be different, don't ever change
have a happy, magical day
have a happy, magical day

There are several play therapy techniques used in healing trauma, and these include the following:

1. Sand Play

This technique gives the child control over their experience by allowing them to build small worlds, scenes, and shapes in a sandbox using small objects.

It gives them an opportunity to process trauma by manifesting it physically in a safe environment.

2. General Play

This method uses old-school playing techniques, toys, games, and imagination, tailoring the tools to the needs of every child to enable them to process their trauma.

3. Drama Therapy

Think of this as a mini-drama school that uses improvisation and drama tools. The child can reenact the trauma as it was, or he could act out scenarios giving different outcomes. This allows the child to tap into their creativity and imagination and approach the problem, solving it in a creative way.

4. Art Therapy

This is a very commonly used technique where the child is asked to recreate their trauma and express their emotions through art and drawing. This way, the child has a sense of control over the experience and helps those who have issues expressing themselves verbally.

5. Gaming Therapy

This is a practice mostly used with children who are reluctant to take part in traditional play. It usually involves the therapist and child interacting while playing a video game together. The child can explore the trauma while playing or relate the game to it, allowing them to feel more in control and comfortable addressing the experience while they're focusing on the game.

6. Nature-Based Play Therapy

Nature plays a core role in play therapy. Most of your happy memories as a child are set in parks, near trees, or in backyards, places where you felt safe and in control. A therapist often uses these places as an escape for the child from their traumatic experience during therapy. Nature-centered play builds stronger resilience, a deeper family connection, and a sense of overall stability as the child engages with the outside natural object in the same way he uses the toys indoors.

Play Therapy Exercises

1. Magic Wand Play

In this game, the therapist hands the child a wand and asks them to think about three wishes they want to come true. Usually, when the child recites the three wishes, one of them will involve real-life troubles that need to be addressed and healed.

2. Puppet Play

This exercise is effective in understanding dynamic relationships. There is a method called the Family puppet, during which each family member, including the traumatized child, is handed a puppet. They are each encouraged to tell a story through the puppet and then are interviewed about the set story. This allows a child to talk about issues within the family that the child is not normally comfortable verbalizing. It is also believed to impact patients afflicted with selective mutism.

3. Clay Play Therapy

In the process of shaping the clay, the child can release any pent-up stress. While they're doing so, they may sculpt a personality that has contributed to their mental health issue, through which the therapist can connect the dots and work out a plan of action.

4. Color Your Life Play Therapy

This is a very effective method that helps the therapist to engage with a child. Children all love colors, don't they? Using this method, the therapist distributes colored items among the contributors. They could be candy, small balls, skittles, or M&Ms, and asks everyone to sort them by color. Each member is asked a set of questions according to the number of each color.

For instance, for every yellow-colored object, describe a happy memory.

For every red-colored item, describe what worries you. And so on.

5. Self-Control Play

There is a well-known and often-used game in the therapeutic community called "Simon Says." Not only does it allow the child to control their emotions, but it also encourages them to pay attention.

The child is asked to follow the commands you give, but only when you say, "Simon Says." This game is good for breaking the ice and creating an air of mirth, which allows the child to open up during physical activity.

6. The Water Bead Sensory Bin

This is a technique that helps calm a child, ease their nerves, and is fun to participate in. The blue and purple colors added to the water bin are soothing and have a relaxing effect. Sometimes to double down on the peacefulness, therapists may add lavender to the water.

7. Communication Games

In this method, the tools used are usually board games with a little bit of a twist.

Like any board game, the children place their tokens at the starting point as the dice are thrown, and each takes their turn. Every time you land on a square, you pick one of three cards: a talking card, a doing card, or a feeling card.

The player follows the instructions on the card, and based on the responses they give, the therapist is able to understand the lingering psychological issues they may be struggling with.

Like any board game, the winner is the one who ends up with the most chips.

8. Guided Imagery

This one is mostly applied to children who have nightmares that they can't shake.

The therapist needs to change how the child looks at the nightmare, like saying it's a movie that can have alternative endings.

The therapist then guides the child through the process of figuring out a better ending to their nightmare.

This exercise allows the child to assume command of their mind.

9. Superhero Play

In this game, the child draws one of their most beloved superheroes, explaining what their superpowers are. Once they've finished, the therapist starts pointing out the similarities in strengths between the character and the child, allowing for a more positive self-image of themselves.

Conclusion

The world is growing at such a fast pace, and there is an ever-increasing need to keep connecting with your child; with time, this may become challenging for you as a parent. As children mature, they develop a sense of dependence on themselves. Toddlers no longer want to be held while walking, preschoolers no longer want to be dressed or cared for by their parents, and teens no longer want to hang around with the family. At every stage, children strive to be heard more than to listen. Being a parent and caregiver, you're meant to grow with them and adapt in every single way. And to do so, you should offer them a safe space to grow by using the Play Therapy Technique.

In Play Therapy, the objective is to reinforce your parent-child relationship and provide you with a rich source of knowledge on how to harness the power of play therapy. Drawing from the latest research on child psychology and development, this book has provided you with practical experiences, offering you a basic yet expert guide on this journey of nurturing the emotional and social growth of your child.

From the early chapters, you're given the most basic explanation of what play therapy entails, and from there, you're shown the different stages of your child's growth (from birth to adolescence) and what you should expect at each stage as a parent. This Play Therapy book doesn't leave you hanging there but lets you in on the power of play therapy at different stages of your child's development. Armed with this knowledge, you can then build a stronger and much more lasting bond with your child.

Now that you've explored the many ways to improve connections with your children, it's time to do the necessary communication. Call them, have brief talks, note your observations, and use the play techniques you've learned. Don't rush, and don't expect to get it all right on your first attempt. You should leave room for mistakes and adjustments both from your end and your child's. Show them that you care and that you're with them every step of the way. For children with disorders and even traumatic experiences, you should know that they'll need more care and attention.

Certainly, you've gained a wealth of wisdom reading this book! Now would be a great time for you to add your reviews of the book so that they can be shared by other parents looking for the same kind of help. Reviews can serve as a means to inspire and encourage others to keep at it. Your review will surely drive others to hop on that train that leads to a lasting and strong friendship with their children!

Lastly, this Play Therapy Guide is combined with guided knowledge from the author and practical exercises and experience to back them up. By using the power of play, you're sure to make a profound impact on your parent-child relationship. Have fun!

Check out another book in the series

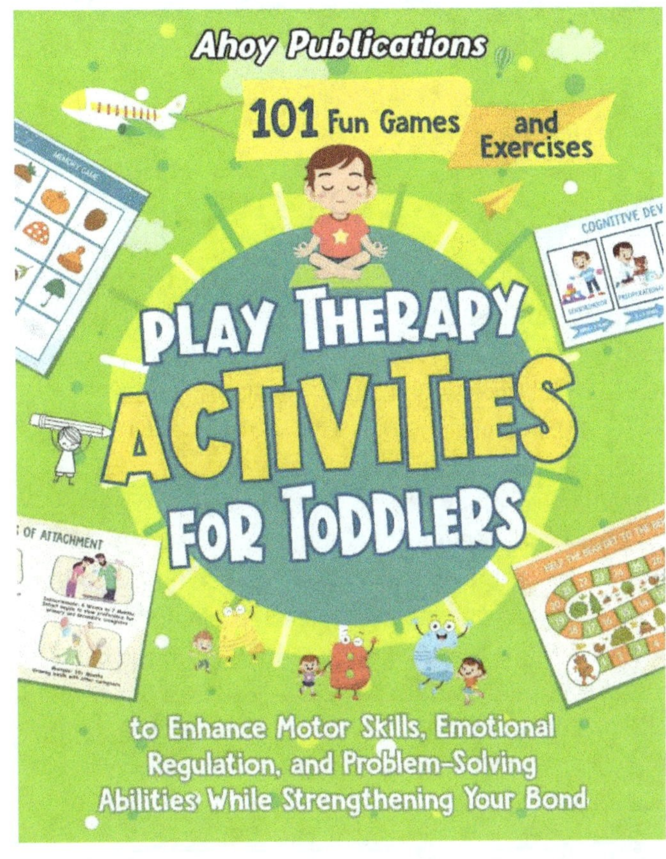

References

10 Fun Sensory Activities for a Child with Autism. (n.d.). Thefca.Co.Uk. https://www.thefca.co.uk/fostering-autistic-children/sensory-activities-children-autism/

20 Evidence-Based Social Skills Activities and Games for Kids. (n.d.). Positiveaction.net. https://www.positiveaction.net/blog/social-skills-activities-and-games-for-kids

25 Play Therapy Techniques. (2020, September 29). Core Wellness CEU Blog. https://www.corewellceu.com/blog/25-play-therapy-techniques/

25 play therapy techniques. (2020, September 29). Core Wellness CEU Blog. https://www.corewellceu.com/blog/25-play-therapy-techniques/

Admin, K. S. W. (2011, May 6). Play and Social Skills. Kid Sense Child Development. https://childdevelopment.com.au/areas-of-concern/play-and-social-skills/

AIPC. (2010, September 29). Developing Social Skills with Play Therapy. Counselling Connection. https://www.counsellingconnection.com/index.php/2010/09/30/developing-social-skills-with-play-therapy/

AmelTherapy, (November 11th, 2021), Play Therapy For Teens? https://ameltherapy.com/blog/2021/11/9/can-play-therapy-work-for-teens

American Academy of Pediatrics, (March 28th, 2019), Stages of Adolescence https://www.healthychildren.org/English/ages-stages/teen/Pages/Stages-of-Adolescence.aspx#:~:text=The%20many%20physical%2C%20sexual%2C%20cognitive,adolescence%20and%20into%20early%20adulthood.

Amy Morin, L. (2018, September 26). Play Therapy. Verywell Family. https://www.verywellfamily.com/what-is-play-therapy-4175560

Benefits of play therapy for children. (n.d.). Betterhelp.com. https://www.betterhelp.com/advice/therapy/play-therapy-for-children-17-benefits/

CEBC » program › child-centered group play therapy ccgpt. (n.d.). Cebc4cw.org. https://www.cebc4cw.org/program/child-centered-group-play-therapy-ccgpt/

Chinekesh, A., Kamalian, M., Eltemasi, M., Chinekesh, S., & Alavi, M. (2013). The effect of group play therapy on social-emotional skills in preschool children. Global Journal of Health Science, 6(2), 163–167. https://doi.org/10.5539/gjhs.v6n2p163

Co., P. (2018, January 16). An age-by-age guide to helping kids manage emotions. The Gottman Institute. https://www.gottman.com/blog/age-age-guide-helping-kids-manage-emotions/

Connections, C. F. C. (2019, May 17). How does play therapy help children heal from trauma? Connections Child & Family Center; Connections Child and Family Center. https://connectionsfamilycenter.com/how-does-play-therapy-help-children-heal-from-trauma/

Cunningham, C. (2023, April 18). 35 Valuable Play Therapy Activities. Teaching Expertise. https://www.teachingexpertise.com/classroom-ideas/play-therapy-activity/

Dewar, G. (2021, September 11). Evidence-based social skills activities for children and teens (with teaching tips). PARENTING SCIENCE; Gwen Dewar. https://parentingscience.com/social-skills-activities/

Fruchter, S. (2017, November 7). Animal-assisted therapy for ASD. ADD & ADHD Holistic Treatment. https://sachscenter.com/animal-assisted-therapy-for-asd/

Frye, D. (2016, September 1). Play Therapy Helps Children with ADHD Build Social Skills. ADDitude. https://www.additudemag.com/play-therapy-may-help-kids-with-adhd-build-social-skills/

Harkin, C. (2019, May 11). Trauma and play therapy. Play Therapy Melbourne. https://www.playtherapymelbourne.com/trauma-and-play-therapy/

Healthline, (October 11th, 2019), by Ann Pietrangelo. How Play Therapy Treats and Benefits Children and Some Adults. https://www.healthline.com/health/play-therapy#when-its-used

How play therapy can help build social skills in children. (n.d.). Wellview Counseling. https://wellviewcounseling.com/how-play-therapy-can-help-build-social-skills-in-children/

How play therapy works –. (n.d.). HEALING TOGETHER. https://www.healingtogetherco.com/how-play-therapy-works

Ilana Danneman, P. T. (n.d.). 10 Gross Motor Skills For Your Child With Autism. Stageslearning.Com. https://blog.stageslearning.com/blog/10-gross-motor-skills-for-your-child-with-autism

Jaganath, N. (n.d.). Children Succeed Autistic Games: Step Into Conversation. Mommy Niri. http://www.mommyniri.com/2009/11/children-succeed-autistic-games-step-into-conversation/

Kennedy Krieger, (2023), Developmental Concerns & Symptoms. https://www.kennedykrieger.org/patient-care/conditions/concerns-symptoms/developmental

Li, P. (2016, December 27). Emotional regulation in children. Parenting For Brain. https://www.parentingforbrain.com/self-regulation-toddler-temper-tantrums/

Lumiere, (January 26th, 2022), 5 Benefits of Play Therapy. https://www.lumierechild.com/lumiere-childrens-therapy/5-benefits-of-play-therapy

masterdaniel. (2021, April 9). Top 10 Social Skill Activities for Autism to Help with Sensory Issues in Children. Special Strong. https://www.specialstrong.com/top-10-social-skill-activities-for-autism-to-help-with-sensory-issues-in-children/

MedicineNet, (November 3rd, 2022), Divya Jacob, Pharm. D. What Are the 5 Stages of Child Development? Signs of Delays. https://www.medicinenet.com/what_are_the_5_stages_of_child_development/article.htm

Mirahmadi, Z., Hemmati Alamdarloo, G., Department of Psychology and Education of Exceptional Children, School of Education & Psychology, University of Shiraz, Shiraz, Iran., & Department of Psychology and Education of Exceptional Children, School of Education & Psychology, University of Shiraz, Shiraz, Iran. (2016). The effectiveness of group play therapy on social skills of female students with intellectual disability. Physical Treatments - Specific Physical Therapy, 6(2), 115–123. https://doi.org/10.18869/nrip.ptj.6.2.115

National Library of Medicine, (1999), Adolescence: A Time of Opportunity and Risk. https://www.ncbi.nlm.nih.gov/books/NBK225165/#:~:text=As%20children%20develop%20into%20adolescents,and%20how%20they%20will%20behave.

Nature-based play therapy as a path to healing for childhood trauma. (2022, September 26). Samuel Centre For Social Connectedness. https://www.socialconnectedness.org/nature-based-play-therapy-as-a-path-to-healing-for-childhood-trauma/

Neurodivergent. (n.d.). Cleveland Clinic. https://my.clevelandclinic.org/health/symptoms/23154-neurodivergent

Parent-Child Relationship – Why it's Important. (2018, October 25). Parenting NI. https://www.parentingni.org/blog/parent-child-relationship-why-its-important/

Pietrangelo, A. (2019, October 11). Play therapy: What is it, how it works, and techniques. Healthline. https://www.healthline.com/health/play-therapy

Play therapy activities for a child with trauma. (2022, January 17). Thefca.co.uk. https://www.thefca.co.uk/what-is-trauma/play-therapy-for-trauma/

Play therapy. (2009, September 15). Goodtherapy.org. https://www.goodtherapy.org/learn-about-therapy/types/play-therapy

Positive relationships for parents and children: how to build them. (2020, August 31). Raising Children Network. https://raisingchildren.net.au/newborns/connecting-communicating/bonding/parent-child-relationships

Pruitt, V. (2023, May 1). Healing through play: The role of play therapy in trauma recovery. Seven Stones Mental Health. https://sevenstonesmentalhealth.com/healing-through-play-the-role-of-play-therapy-in-trauma-recovery/

Pubmed Center, (February 5th, 2005), Deborah Christie, Adolescent development. https://www.ncbi.nlm.nih.gov/pmc/articles/PMC548185/#:~:text=During%20adolescence%20young%20people%20will,of%20emotional%2C%20personal%2C%20and%20financial

Rouse, M. H. (2016, October 31). How can we help kids with self-regulation? Child Mind Institute. https://childmind.org/article/can-help-kids-self-regulation/

Short, J. (1487730705000). Top seven challenges in counseling children. Linkedin.com. https://www.linkedin.com/pulse/top-seven-challenges-counselling-children-jacki-short

Sutton, J. (2017, July 27). Play therapy: What is it, and how does it work? Positivepsychology.com. https://positivepsychology.com/play-therapy/

Sutton, J. (2017, July 27). Play therapy: What is it and how does it work? Positivepsychology.com. https://positivepsychology.com/play-therapy/

Sutton, J. (2017, July 27). Play Therapy: What Is It and How Does It Work? Positivepsychology.com. https://positivepsychology.com/play-therapy/

Sutton, J. (2022, November 3). 28 best therapy games for healing through play. Positivepsychology.com. https://positivepsychology.com/therapy-games/

Trauma-informed play therapy. (n.d.). My Site. https://www.kiefercounselingct.com/trauma-informed-play-therapy

West, S. (2019, July 3). Expressive play therapy for healing complex trauma. Centre for Expressive Therapy. https://centreforexpressivetherapy.com/expressive-play-therapy-for-healing-complex-trauma/

What does a Play Therapist do? (n.d.). Birmingham City University. https://www.bcu.ac.uk/education-and-social-work/about-us/school-blog/what-does-a-play-therapist-do

What you need to know about parent-child attachment. (n.d.). Unicef.org. https://www.unicef.org/parenting/child-care/what-you-need-know-about-parent-child-attachment

YouthLight. (n.d.). Using Play Therapy to Develop Social-Emotional Skills – YouthLight Connect. Youthlight.com. https://www.youthlight.com/connect/using-play-therapy-to-develop-social-emotional-skills

www.ingramcontent.com/pod-product-compliance
Lightning Source LLC
Chambersburg PA
CBHW081339120626
46546CB00011B/3412
* 9 7 8 1 9 6 1 2 1 7 4 9 2 *